GRANDPARENTING
A new challenge

First published in 1994 by
Sally Milner Publishing Pty Ltd
558 Darling Street
Rozelle NSW 2039
Australia

© Hélène Gonski 1994

Cover and design by Gretta Kool
Cover photograph by Cathryn Townsend
Illustrations by Amanda Upton
Author's photograph by Benjamin Huie
Colour Separation by Litho Platemakers, South Australia
Printed in Australia by The Book Printer

National Library of Australia
Cataloguing-in-Publication data:

Gonski, Hélène.
    Grandparenting

    ISBN 1 86351 131 8

    1. Grandparenting. 2. Grandparent and child. I. Title.

306.8745

All rights reserved. No part of this publication may be reproduced, stored in a retrieval system or transmitted in any form or by any means, electronic, mechanical, photocopying, recording or otherwise, without prior written permission of the copyright owners and publishers.

To my Grandchildren

Acknowledgements

I feel very privileged that so many grandparents, adult children and grandchildren have shared a great deal of their thoughts and ideas with me. Many thanks to you all. I have not mentioned anyone by their real name in the book, but have used pseudonyms. I have included age only to emphasise a point or stage.

I would like to thank the children at Launceston Church Grammar School and Sydney Grammar School (Edgecliff) for their wonderful drawings and for permitting me to visit their classrooms. Thank you to the teachers, Martin Rossleigh, and my son, Stephen Gonski, for their co-operation and support.

Thank you to Adrienne Katz for her unwavering faith in this book and her valuable ideas and expertise from the UK.

Thank you to my daughter, Lisa, for giving me some wonderfully creative ideas and lots of encouragement.

Thank you to Jetty Windt, who has co-led groups with me and shared a great deal of her knowledge and skills.

Thank you to Renée Durbach, for her support and ability to listen endlessly to my difficulties.

Thank you to my sons, David and Peter, for their interest — and to my 10 grandchildren, who are a sheer joy, and have certainly provided me with much of the material for the book.

And thank you to my husband, Alec, who has been extremely encouraging, and for his ability to cope with an empty fridge and a disorganised household for many months.

I have acknowledged my sources at the end of this book, and sincerely regret any I may have inadvertnetly omitted.

My grandfather teaching me how to ride.
Christopher (9 yrs)

Foreword

The seeds of this book were sown in the fertile soil of the Later Years and Grandparenting groups in which I have been involved for some years. Unlike parenthood, where there is a choice, grandparenthood is thrust upon us. My interest was stimulated by the group members who have been reflecting on this role and also by my own tentativeness in relating to my endearing and lively grandchildren.

I have deliberately done little formal research so that I could get a more personal viewpoint. I have gone into classrooms to hear what grandchildren have to say, and also listened to many grandparents and adult children. I hope that the book will serve to supplement the knowledge and skills that grandparents already have.

The focus of this book is on the building of good relationships. This requires an understanding of the needs of others and how to help them and, at the same time, learning to look after ourselves.

The book also debunks the myths, still prevailing, that grandparents are wizened, fragile or authoritarian old people. On the contrary, they have become younger and more active and stand on the brink of something new.

Grandchildren present opportunities for new relationships and a chance to explore and understand the changes in our modern world. They provide us with some of our most tender and loving moments and, without a doubt, some of our funniest times.

Grandparents are invaluable for the time, attention and love they can give. Their wisdom and experience of the past contribute to the continuity of life.

As we go into the 21st century, I believe that grandparents have a unique part to play in helping today's adult children and grandchildren prepare for the future. They can highlight to the world, a need for the revival of the extended family if we are to overcome the fragility and fragmentation of our communities.

Gran and Papa playing draughts
Jono (7 yrs)

CHAPTER 1
Sailing on Uncharted Waters

*t*he telephone rings. The news breaks. My grandchild has arrived. There is much excitement and celebration. At hospital, the room is festooned with flowers, balloons and cards. My heart melts at the sight of the baby. Then reality sets in, and I ponder my role. What do I do? Where do I fit in? How do I make a good relationship? What is expected of a grandparent? How much time will I give?.

These were some of the questions I asked myself when my first grandchild was born. I looked up 'grandparent' in the dictionary. The meaning is 'parent of a parent'. That seemed quite logical. However, the 'grand' part bothered me. Super, splendid, sound, important, great, dignified, noble and proud were some of the meanings mentioned. Quite daunting, I thought.

When I approached the librarian for material on

grandparenting, she looked at me blankly. 'Grandparenting? Isn't that the same as parenting?' Hardly, I muttered to myself. She looked through the computer index and came up with nothing. 'Anyway, doesn't everyone know how to be a grandparent?' she asked.

Chronologically grandparents come before parents. Strange that self-help books abound on every conceivable subject except grandparenting. And there is a vast difference between a parent and a grandparent. I realised I would just have to muddle through and do the best I could.

Being a grandparent is like being a parent a second time around, and so it is a chance to do better than before. There is less agonising over decisions, less restrictions and reduced responsibility. You can hand the grandchildren back to their parents at the end of the day, put your feet up and sip a well-earned drink. Also, emotions are not pulled in quite so many directions and it is possible to be more detached. You can see things more objectively and be looking from the outside in. Grandparenthood can add a great deal of richness to life.

Grandparents are a living link to the past, providing some continuity in putting down roots and giving shelter. The average lifespan has increased and the number of grandparents who are now living longer has also increased. In years gone by, children had only a small chance of having and knowing their grandparents. Today, one out of six children under 15 has a chance of having four or more grandparents still alive. So, for many people, grandparenthood lasts longer and with the upsurge of younger grandparents, it is an experience not just of older age but also middle age.

Nowadays, there seems to be a renewal of this ancient relationship which we need to foster and cherish. In fact, grandparents are now back in fashion as parents experience enormous tensions in our pressured world and often need a helping hand. They may go through difficulties with families, neighbours, jobs, money, housing and health.

In the United States, a Grandparents' Day now exists and is celebrated on the first Sunday after Labor Day. Needless to say, the commercial side, that is, cards and flowers is flourishing. However, the thought is genuinely there, as it is in schools here in Australia. A day is set aside for grandparents to be acknowledged and included; at the same time they can be given a chance to applaud and marvel at the achievements of their grandchildren. Puffing up with pride and boasting is quite acceptable.

A NEW WORLD

The world is changing rapidly. Sometimes I think we are sailing on uncharted waters. In the fifties, when I reared four children, ignorance was bliss and we muddled through. Times are very different now and changes can be very perplexing and confusing.

Babies clad in navy and red go everywhere. They travel to Europe, change library books, visit concert halls and are keen shoppers in the supermarkets. Five-year-olds hold opinions on the major issues of the day. The cost of the tooth fairy has risen to a dollar a tooth. This is quite considerable when I have to multiply 20 teeth by 10 grandchildren! At the age of seven, or earlier, children are adept at computers, they are virtuoso violinists, Wimbledon tennis champions and aspiring Michelangelos. Eleven-year olds start dating and can digest the most adult films and books. Teenagers design their own clothes and go to discos and clubs. Communication is not exactly easy. It is quite complex being a grandparent when the world is on the move, and there are so many changes in different areas. Grandparents can feel buffeted about and find it hard to secure a place in a family of three or four generations.

THEN AND NOW

Today, relationships with grandchildren differ a great deal from the past. When asked what is different, today's grandparents maintain that their grandparents had been authoritarian figures — patriarchs and matriarchs. They were held in awe and respect, and ruled the family. The idea of getting down on the floor, or being on the children's level was out of the question. Horsing around, playing cowboys and indians, would have caused an uproar. I recall a photograph of my grandfather, dressed in his best suit and hat, sitting very tentatively on an antique chair placed in the garden while we sat at his feet. Now there is equality, companionship, honesty and less emotional distance. The relationship is much closer and less formal and isn't concerned only with the physical welfare of the children. As Cherlin and Furstenberg say in their book *The American Grandparent*, the grandparent relationship has become more 'companionate' based on family ties and sentiment. There is less authority and less financial power.

Mae says, 'In our day, grandparents never had the interest. Today we like to see our grandchildren grow up and be part of our lives. We like to listen, love and spoil them'. Others say their grandparents were remote, cranky, formidable and often unknown. Distances were often great between families and there was little available transport for frequent visits. Visits to grandparents were often regarded with trepidation.

One grandmother said, 'Although I went to my grandparents for holidays I got no affection, or cuddles, or sat on anyone's knee. Nobody said I was special'. Only a few in the group mentioned any positive experiences; one grandmother said, 'Grandmother seemed old to me in her strange dress, but I suppose I loved her in a detached way'. Peter, the grandfather of three, maintained that his grandparents knew far more than he, but now he feels his computer-literate grandchildren are way ahead of him. A humbling feeling. Barbara said that her family are all teachers and she feels very inferior. She describes herself as 'just a housewife'. Children are tending to outstrip their grandparents educationally, but what the latter contribute doesn't depend on a university degree. The loving, caring and affection cannot be measured — nor can the wisdom, experience and common sense.

Today, families are smaller and it is easier to get around to all the members. My mother was one of 14 children. There was no way that my grandparents could reach out and form relationships with all their grandchildren, let alone their children. Stories abound of my mother and her siblings getting lost, nearly drowning in waterholes, falling off horses and the usual accidents and pranks of children — and this multiplied by 14! For my mother's generation, the roles of parenting and grandparenting overlapped as they played dual roles. Grandparenting would have had a blurred identity.

CHANGING GRANDPARENTS

Before World War II, life expectancy was much lower than today. Today, grandparents are more active and healthier, with time and energy to give. They work fewer hours, or are retired and able to give love and affection in a closer way. Perhaps the role of mentor has lessened, but there is more chance for good and warm relationships. Younger grandparents are growing in numbers and have challenging careers and jobs. More will be said about them in the chapter on 'baby boomers'. (See Chapter 9.)

The following poem illustrates the changing grandmother — but it could also apply to grandfathers. The author is unknown, but is obviously a grandchild.

Thoroughly Modern Granny

I have a little granny, she's really very old,
But also unconventional in a most unusual mould.
She doesn't wear her spectacles perched upon her nose,
She is into contact lenses and varnishes her toes.
Unlike some other grannies who are home before dark,
She's dressed up in a tracksuit and jogging in the park.
And when I wish she'd sometimes stay and tuck me into bed,
She's off to study yoga and standing on her head.
Some grannies sit in rocking chairs and crochet shawls indoors,
My granny jumps upon a horse and rides across the moors.
She goes on day trips with her gang - the over-sixties club,
They rocket round the countryside and end up in the pub.
And on the homeward journey, like a flock of singing birds,
They harmonise old favourites with very naughty words.
I love my little granny, I think she's really great,
If that's what growing old is like, I simply cannot wait.

ENVIRONMENT

How the environment has changed. The sea is polluted, the forests and the ozone layer depleted and the air can be toxic. Walking along the beach can be quite hazardous. Blue bottle jellyfish, with their menacing threads, lie on the shore. And, of course, lying in the sun has become a no-no, even in colder climates. Up north, in beautiful Queensland, the box jellyfish and the crown-of-thorns starfish mar the beauty of the reef. In the backyard, touching shrubs like the brightly coloured rhus tree can have disastrous effects on the skin. Patting the household cat can precipitate a bout of asthma and scabies, we are told, is here for the next 15 years. The only way to combat it is to have no human contact! What about picking up ticks as you take your early morning stroll on a fresh spring morning? No wonder that at a school concert the children sang:

> *We are a rock revolving around a golden sun,*
> *We are a billion children rolled into one,*
> *So when I hear about a hole in the sky,*
> *Salt water wells in my eyes.*

There is overcrowding; now we have high-rise housing with little space for children to run and play. Quite a different picture from the small towns and villages that many of the elders came from. Riding a bicycle, or walking freely, still exists but not to the same degree. I can remember 20 years ago, sleeping with a ground-floor sliding door open to the outside. It was safe for children to hitchhike and go to the cinema on their own. Today, high walls and burglar alarms are commonplace and crime is on the rise. For parents, it is a hard to know when to protect children and when to let them be independent. Letting them go by themselves on a bus to school, or walk alone to the shops can be a dilemma.

WORK AND CHILDCARE

Today, often both parents are working. They come home tired and drained and are faced with household chores and any number of school activities. There is also intense competition in the work force and it is often a struggle to survive.

Childcare is not always available and when it is, it can

be enormously costly.

Even very young children go into day care. Seeing little babies all dressed for their daily program is sometimes hard to accept, but parents frequently have no option. Grandparents can be called upon to help, particularly when there is sickness or a crisis. Psychologist, Lilian Troll, maintains that grandparents provide a service as 'family watchdogs'. They look out for trouble and provide assistance.

VALUES

Material prosperity goes forward despite recessions and there is a different value placed on money. It is so often regarded as a god and the market place its temple. Cupboards bulge with a variety of toys, sportsgear and clothes. Huge amounts are spent on supplying the needs of the family. This is sometimes difficult to accept for older people who have struggled all their lives. After World War II, there was an era of permissiveness when it wasn't always realised that along with personal freedom comes personal responsibility. Nowadays, life is frenetic and time out is a luxury. A sense of not belonging has lead to the advent of cults and the taking of drugs. Value is placed more on what children do, rather than on who they are as people.

Values can conflict about religion, smoking, entertainment, health, hygiene and any number of issues. Beth didn't like her grandsons having boxing lessons. Her son felt she could be more encouraging but her values were different and she couldn't be dishonest. She agreed not to protest and to accept their choice as long as she didn't have to watch.

The role of a parent, the most important role in the world, is not given sufficient acknowledgement. The job is a 24-hour one with no pay and no holidays. It can be extremely stressful. If they are able to offer their time, grandparents can be models for their values of loving, caring and accepting. Such examples are often a scarce commodity in our world today.

FAMILY

The divorce rate is high, one in three marriages break up in some countries. Households and families are continually changing. This can be extremely difficult for grandparents and their relationships with grandchildren. Second marriages often do not survive. Step-parents and single parents are on the increase and today's idea of the family bears little semblance to the ideas of the past. In some cases it had changed its composition and today a family is regarded as a group of people who strive to care for each other, to find some happiness.

PARENTING

There have been many changes in the way people live and work. In the past, children were seen and not heard. Queen Victoria loved her family from a distance. Modern parents are more honest and open with their families. Children say what they think and are given a sense of equality. Way back, I heard a parent say, 'If you mention that word again I'll wash your mouth out with soap.' Today, language is free and four-letter words appear to be part of the vocabulary. Teenagers also sprinkle their talk with 'cool', 'awesome', 'radical', 'dude' and 'nerd'.

Life is more informal and children participate in everything. Parents go to classes on parenting and read numerous books. There can be 20 different opinions on how to rear a family — whether to burp or not to burp; to use a dummy or not; to breastfeed or not; to discipline or not; to give girls trucks and boys dolls. So many choices: it can be quite confusing.

The ways of bringing up families have changed and, at times, this can be a hard pill to swallow. Perhaps we, the older generation, don't agree and struggle to keep quiet. We may feel that too many expectations are put onto children. They can have an overload of information too quickly or too early, which can eventuate in a child becoming an adult far too soon. After school, activities are frenetic. Parents chauffeur their children in all directions; there is hardly a moment for just fun and play. Tiredness abounds as families collapse into bed at late hours. This type of parenting seems foreign to us but perhaps, in time, we can learn something new and accept the differences.

DIET

Diet is different today and fast foods, icecream, sweets and chips are the order of the day. For the sophisticated, there are olives, salami and pickles. I often wonder how children can survive on so many foods that lack nourishment. Some children have five meals a day, mostly containing a great deal of junk ingredients. A balanced diet has gone out the window and yet children look reasonably healthy and exceedingly well padded, on the whole. Warnings are given about obesity — one in three young Australians are overweight. Research has shown that, by the age 45, those who were fat as adolescents had already begun to die sooner than those who were not overweight in their teens. By the age of 70 twice as many had died as normal. On the other hand, there is the waif look, when children want to be as thin as possible. This attitude is exacerbated by the media, which portrays images of beauty that encourage young people to find fault with themselves. Young girls are encouraged to diet to fit into beautiful clothes rather than to purchase clothes suitable for their size. Apparently, one in ten children go to school without breakfast, especially in the lower income areas, and are found to be deficient in calcium and iron. Others go off munching chocolate bars.

There are also many food fads. Peter, aged five, loved to go to MacDonalds but he only ate the bun not the meat. Jeremy refused to eat his meal. It appeared that it was contaminated by a lettuce leaf! James would only eat a soya bean hamburger. Grandparents tell stories of their grandchildren turning up their noses at the wrong sort of butter or cheese, or if the meat is too raw or too well done for their taste. It is often hard for those grandparents who lived through the Great Depression to see food thrown in the bin. Their programming is to eat everything on the plate, no matter what. And, of course, this was not always very palatable. I recall my boarding-school days, and having to face grey vegetables drowning in water (this has turned me off vegetables ever since). As a result, my family complained of a vegetable deprivation when they were growing up. This is a reaction to negative experiences of the past and is certainly not the answer when feeding the family.

Today, there are often no definite times to eat, and families generally do not sit down together. Mealtime conversation is impossible as family members race in different directions and food is no longer to do with love or a connecting link. This seems to depict the rootlessness of the modern family as people grab fast foods on the move. Someone I know maintains that his daughter-in-law is queen of the takeaways! For some, cooking is a thing of the past.

Mealtimes can also be delayed when parents work. Sometimes, it is nine o'clock before dinner is ready. This can conflict with the views of grandparents who can see that the children are hungry and irritable. Grandparents can give suggestions or offer practical help, if wanted. Otherwise, they need to realise and accept that this is the way this family operates.

Maybe we can adopt a healthier lifestyle by shopping for fruit, vegetables and low-fat foods. Together, with parents, we can be models for better living and eating, and encourage the old ritual of mealtimes to start again.

DRESS

There is an informality regarding the dress of the day. No frock coats and crinolines, hoops or bustles. More likely jeans, crazy tee-shirts and multicoloured hair. Hats are not only worn outside but indoors as well, for some unknown reason. There is a sense of comfort. In fact, anything goes.

DIFFERENCE AND SAMENESS

There are so many changes in the world around us. Grandparents have witnessed man on the moon, the advent of television, computers, the contraceptive pill, compact discs and Kylie Minogue's uplift bra. The list goes on. *Grandmother's Chair,* by Ann Scott Herbert and Meg Kelleher, highlights changes through three generations but also stresses continuity and some sameness. It is the story of three girls who sat on the same special chair. First, the great-grandmother, then the grandmother and, lastly, the mother. Pictures of old-fashioned rag dolls, forties-style radio, and sixties-style television denote the passage of time. What remains the same are the stars seen through the window, the love of the parents and the old friendly chair. These are some constants in a changing world.

SHIFTING ATTITUDES

People are now living longer and, in Australia, 11.15 per cent of the population are older than 65 and the number of 80-year-olds has doubled in the last 30 years. Seventy per cent of these are women as a woman's life expectancy is 80 years and a man's 75. Adult children's attitudes are beginning to shift: in the past, they may have resented help, but now they are more likely to welcome some assistance. Both parents are often working and are overstretched. In the break-up of the traditional family group there is a need for an anchor. Grandparents, who are now more active and younger, have a bigger part to play. They can be a significant source of help for the family in good times and in bad. There is now more emphasis on healthy ageing rather than the unhealthy aspects. Hopefully, older people are not necessarily seen as weak, frail and dependent. There have been tremendous advances in longevity, fitness, alertness and education.

ALTERNATIVE LIVING

There are still grandparents who feel they have been failures as child rearers and, consequently, keep themselves in the adult-only worlds. All the childcare books and experts help to consolidate the feeling of inadequacy and uselessness. Also, in the adult-only world they only need to look after themselves and have the freedom to do as they wish. Communities of older citizens have grown, particularly in the US where, it appears, grandparents are having a wow of a time, relaxing in jacuzzis and Californian hot tubs. Their lives are busy and fulfilled and they see their grandchildren only at certain specified times. This appears to work well for them, even though Betty Friedan describes this type of living as 'playpens for the aged'.

In Australia, it seems that retirement villages for the over-fifty-fives are mushrooming. People in these homes feel liberated from responsibilities, safe and secure. And there is some comfort in living near your peers who understand where you are at in life. There is also more independence and less reliance on family and friends — no having to wait for someone to change the light bulb, or carry a weighty parcel or mow the lawn. It is, however, a matter of individual choice and not everybody's cup of tea. This kind of lifestyle may also be isolating from the community and it is easy to miss out on the generation mix.

Some retirement villages have glossy, unrealistic advertisements that show residents brimming with health and smiling broadly. They appear to be on the go and soaking up all the comfort of the amenities. However, there must be some 'rainy days'. Those in the luxury accommodation are called Woopies (well-off older people) — are they at last making whoopy? There are also budget-class villages, run by church bodies, which are becoming more and more popular.

In these situations, grandparents can have their grandchildren visit, or do the visiting themselves when it suits. The decision rests with them whether village life is what they want and how they will keep the interchange between generations. This can be a good arrangement as long as they are not conned into it by commercial enterprise, or made to feel they are unwanted — they need to be aware of what they are taking on for there is a real danger of being exploited. People have lost large amounts of money and family contacts.

INTERCHANGE

Interchange between generations can be so rewarding. My

grandchildren have given me a sense of renewal and lots of fun and laughter. I have also been introduced to many new things, including Nintendos (a mixed blessing), computer words like disks, drives and bytes, new rules in hockey, modern music and novel ways of dressing. I was kicking a soccer ball in our backyard with my grandson, aged seven. 'Granny,' he said, 'your kicks are so high, you could be a goalkeeper in our team.' Quite a compliment. I also wouldn't have believed I would be whirling around in a large teacup in Disneyland and trying valiantly to stomach a gobstopper!

Contact between generations gives the young an opportunity to get acquainted with older people and vice versa. This can help to break down the age barriers and create a very valuable 'two-way street.'

SO MANY HATS

Grandparents come in all sizes, shapes and ages. Grandparents wear many hats. Firstly, as a babysitter, although, whoever sits? More likely, it is to be on the move, in Reeboks and tracksuits. Or as a chauffeur, with endless trips to football, soccer, tennis, piano, gym, and the like. Or storyteller. I often wonder how many times the three little pigs have had their houses blown down? What about a photographer, consoler, teacher, companion or magician? How about a baker? In our family, the tradition for birthdays is the making of cup cakes, iced with garish colours and topped with hundreds and thousands (a recipe from a great-grandmother). What about as a carpenter? Feverish calls from the grandchildren to make shields for their knights or houses for their beetles. In the acting business, I recall snorting like a pig and going through the antics of Old Macdonald having a farm. And, perhaps most important of all, having over-sized ears to listen and a large heart to give unconditional love.

All this can be somewhat daunting. There are so many roles to play and a dearth of information in bookshops, the media and the world. The material in this book is to add to the wealth of natural skills and wisdom that grandparents already have. Nobody wants to be told what to do or how to live. People have different viewpoints and ways of coping. If something works well there is no need to change it. However, in the chapters to come, you have a choice of doing something different if it fits your style and personality.

Forming, and then enriching, relationships with grandchildren and adult children is of prime importance. 'According to the best of my remembrance my grandmother was the wickedest and the worst woman that ever lived.' This is a quote from Charles Dickens in *Hard Times*. We hardly want to hear that from our grandchildren. Grandparenting is a special relationship and fills in the gap that often exists in families. It can range from being a walking tuckshop, to being a very good friend.

INGREDIENTS FOR A GOOD RELATIONSHIP

- Motivation to be there and give some time.
- Listening to the other person and offering support.
- Looking after your own rights.
- A dollop of fun and humour.

All this needs to be sprinkled with a large amount of love, caring, honesty and openness.

Children often think their grandparents lived in a time before time began. This was illustrated by Jono, aged six, speaking to his grandfather.

Jono: Were you in Noah's Ark?
Grandfather: No.
Jono: Then why weren't you drowned?

Grandparents have an enormous part to play in our uncertain world. They can also help to fill in this time warp between generations and model a more gentle, productive and positive way of ageing.

In the following chapters, I will suggest some skills in dealing with relationships, particularly with grandchildren and adult children. Good communication and an acceptance of others is very important. At the same time, we need to look at how we are regarded by society and how to empower ourselves in order to debunk some of the myths. Having fun, enjoyment and enrichment is a vital part of grandparenthood — together with lots of laughter. If we could only bottle the latter, what a wonder drug it would be!

Even though the world has changed so much, there are ways of fairer sailing on those uncharted waters.

Out sailing
Ben (6 yrs)

CHAPTER 2
Myths and Realities

When you think of the alternative getting old isn't so bad.
Maurice Chevalier

Our society idolises the young and often denigrates older people. This is often different in other cultures, where old people are cared for by family and revered for their wisdom and knowledge. With the Aborigines, people are respected when they become grey and are gifted with magical powers. In Asia, older people become the philosophers — in China, grandparents are greatly respected by their children and grandchildren and often live together in three-generation families. In the US, the Navajo Indians' medicine men start to train only when they are older, believing that they are wiser then. In Italy, and other parts of Europe, families can be close and grandparents have an important influence.

In our culture, when somebody says 'you look so young' it is meant as a compliment. The word 'old' is an insult. Old is considered ugly and young beautiful. Ageism usually implies negative attitudes to ageing; the public image of elders is often undermining. It is understandable that, for some, going into the later years has an uncomfortable connotation.

I will be mentioning people's age in years as I go on in the book, just to illustrate the myths, but I am generally of the belief that it is unnecessary to focus on the age of a person at all.

When I was asked to give a talk on the later years, I was told not to make it too depressing. The audience wouldn't like it. They wanted to be cheered up not saddened. What makes the subject of ageing so dreary? How accurate are society's views on ageing? There is even some difficulty in labelling older people — elderly, retirees, oldsters, old-age pensioners, golden oldies, veterans, seniors, old fogeys, wrinklies, oldies, over-the-hillers, geriatrics (do we call someone who goes to an obstetrician an obstetric?) How often are older people seen as a fund of knowledge and wisdom? Do we frown on older people dressed in jeans and younger styled clothes? 'Mutton dressed up as lamb', is whispered around the room.

If we think of age to age, we can divide our lives into four parts.

1. The First Age is the nappy to adolescence period of childhood dependence.
2. The Second Age is parental responsibility and being employed full-time.
3. The Third Age is retirement and developing post-work activity. Between 1991 and 2011, there will be an expected increase in the population group, aged 60 years and over, of between 16 and 20 per cent. It is believed that an active Third Age can postpone dependency.

4. The Fourth Age is the time of dependence and withdrawal. (From Peter Laslett's book, *A Fresh Map of Life*.)

The ages of grandparents vary from 40-year-olds (sometimes even younger) right into the eighties, but the majority are in their later years. We cannot turn back the clock but we can control our participation in the process of ageing and dispel a lot of the myths.

Thinking of grandparents often conjures up a picture of a white-haired woman with a bun, spectacles on her nose, knitting in a rocking chair, or a bumbling semi-bald man with gnarled fingers, tottering up the garden path. The reality is more likely to be an active person in Reeboks and tracksuit, a keen golfer, enthusiastic traveller, walker, politician, worker or writer.

Recently, a festival for grandparents was held in Bono Arctic, Norway. Activities included horse riding, parachute jumping, scuba diving and soccer, as well as concerts and theatre performances. In Japan, twin sisters of 99 are the latest pop music sensation and, in the US, 97-year-old Beatrice is pictured in a book of photography hula-hooping! Anything is possible.

At age 78, Grandma Moses (Anna Mary) started to paint in oils when her fingers became too stiff to manipulate a needle for her embroidery. This opened up a whole new career for her for which she became famous. Her paintings were primitive and brightly coloured and expressed her memories of 'Old Timey' farm life in New York and Virginia. She died at the age of 101.

Picasso defied tradition by painting in his nineties and fathering a child at the same time. Charlie Chaplin was still directing at 78 and having a busy family life. Arthur Rubinstein gave one of his best musical recitals at 89 after an eye operation, relying almost entirely on his memory.

Freya Stark, the British travel writer, was climbing the Himalayas at 90. Examples in history are endless.

Coming closer to home, Dot Butler, 82, was abseiling over the Sydney Harbour bridge to launch 'Age Adds Value' week. Lloyd Rees was painting pictures, awash with light, at 92. Ruth Cracknell, 68, a grandmother of five, won a Sydney Opera House Award for her acting. She is still appearing in the television series *Mother and Son*. Colleen Clifford, the Australian actor, won an award at 96 for her contribution to the entertainment world. The list goes on. What about the infamous granny who fraudently received ten pension cheques at once and complained that she wasn't being paid enough money? Older people are even making their mark in crime. Then there are 'ordinary' older people who are carers, parents, grandparents and workers and who need to be recognised in society.

There is a myth that older people lose their 'marbles'. They are considered to be unproductive, powerless and dependent. It is said they have rigid personalities, that they are egocentric, selfish and asocial. Their irritability, forgetfulness and fearfulness are often mentioned. Have you not met young people with the same traits? None of these characteristics are exclusive to the later years. The prejudices about old age often poison the minds of the community.

Ageing is sometimes seen as an illness. But ageing is not synonymous with disease, but is normal part of the human life cycle. There are, of course, many degenerative illnesses, such as heart disease, cancer and arthritis, that occur more frequently in the later years but they are due to pathological processes and entirely separate from normal ageing. An 'aged' person is someone who has been there longer than a young person and is not to be thrown on the scrap heap.

A man in his seventies went to the doctor. 'My knee is very sore and I find it hard to walk.' The doctor said, 'What do you expect at your age?' The man answered, 'But my other knee is the same age and it doesn't hurt at all.' He was given good medical attention but the attitude needed changing. His other knee was healthy, despite his age.

Hopefully, today's community will place an emphasis on healthy ageing, rather than on the ills, saying it is too late for preventive care. In the past, health promotion and disease prevention for the older person have been sadly neglected.

FROM THE MEDIA

The media is a powerful exponent of myths. From what we see on television, we are led to believe that elders don't brush their teeth or shampoo their hair, and are not active enough to use deodorants. The advertisements show older people popping pain pills, making telephone calls to other countries, or reading by the fireside. Apparently they don't drink Coca-Cola, eat tasty pasta, read books, travel or use household products. In fact, it looks as if they are not engaged in anything interesting. They are depicted as very passive. And they are not regarded as a lucrative source of purchasing power. Only at Christmas time do advertisements focus on older people, to encourage them to buy toys for grandchildren – in the US, it appears that 25 per cent of toys are bought by grandparents. In 1983, only 4 per cent of older people were featured in television programs and today it isn't that much higher. Magazines and books endorse this negative attitude. In literature for children, grandparents are often ridiculed or regarded as selfish grumpy people.

DEBUNKING THE MYTHS

Grandparenthood can be a great fund of strength and vitality. We need to free ourselves from stereotypical thinking. As Bernard Baruch said, 'To me, old age is always 15 years older than I am.'

As is sometimes suggested, ageing doesn't need to be a problem for the country's health resources. On the contrary. A survey conducted in England by the Policy Institute found that 36 per cent of women returning to work left their children with grandmothers. Are grandmothers becoming an exploited, overworked and underpaid group? In Australia, 43 per cent of grandmothers provide informal childcare, and 76 per cent of all grandparents are engaged in some form of childminding. Their contribution challenges some of the myths but it is often dismissed. Jill happily cared for her grandchild, aged 18 months, for four days a week. She maintained that her daughter would not have been able to work without her help as childcare was too expensive. I spotted Carol pushing her grandchild up the hill in a trolley with all the supermarket shopping. She looked as if she were playing martyr, as she was quite resentful about minding her grandson all day. Whichever way you look at it, older people have become an immense resource for the community and one wonders what would happen if grandparents started to demand their rights? In other words, money and recognition for all the work they do.

Grandparents help with first homes, buying furniture, and helping young families on their way. They are out and about working, shopping, relaxing in clubs, studying, doing paid or voluntary work and being active in community life.

In reasonable health, grandparents can expect 20 years or more of good quality life after their working life has finished. Inside, they feel just the same as they ever did, only now they have grandparent faces. Ned said that he didn't feel that different from 35 years ago, when he walked down the aisle to be married. Others feel they have moved on physically, emotionally, mentally and socially – a type of evolution to another stage which can be productive.

It is a myth that older people have sexual hangups or aren't interested in continuing with their sex lives. They can enjoy sex right into the later years. Active young lovers become active old lovers, with no fear of pregnancy. There may be a decline in frequency and interest, a biological change but not necessarily in feeling. Betty, an adult, was shocked to see her grandmother in the engaged column of the newspaper. Equally, so was Len, who couldn't see why his mother was getting married again — after all, she had 10 grandchildren! 'Wasn't she too old for that sort of thing?'

MYTHS & REALITIES
(from the point-of-view of adult children & grandchildren)

Lack of frequent contact with older people leads to a paucity of knowledge about them and from this prejudices can arise. Some women are having children in their late thirties and the grandchildren have a shorter time to relate to their grandparents. I migrated with four small children and they never really had an opportunity to to know their grandparents, or even to have any experiences with older people. It was a loss for them and for me, and a cut-off from the generation of elders.

Grandchildren are often influenced by fairytales and stories where grandparents are depicted in derogatory ways. 'She was a selfish, grumpy old woman. She had pale brown teeth and a small puckered-up mouth like a dog's bottom.' This comes from *George's Marvellous Medicine* by Roald Dahl. School books can also tend to show Granny with a tight grey-haired bun, slopping around in slippers, and Grandpa wielding a stick and looking very fierce. What about Spike Milligan's first verse of *Granny*?

> *Through every nook and every cranny*
> *The wind blew in on poor old Granny*
> *Around her knees, into each ear*
> *(And up her nose as well I fear.)*

Rather black humour — but the children roar with laughter.

Grandchildren's perception of grandparents

I got some 10-year-olds to draw their grandparents. They drew them with little or no hair, gold teeth, spectacles, smudged lipstick and wrinkles. Some had big smiles, others had down-turned mouths. Most of the pictures were very large and showed their grandparents enjoying themselves — playing chess, boating, baking, golfing, swimming, or watching television. They were wearing loose, casual clothes, the implication was that grandparents don't work. Some were in warm woollies so as not to get cold.

The children were very perceptive as there is a myth that all grandparents are alike. However, some have a sense of humour and are active, some are serious and quiet, others are restless, cranky, critical or loving. Some are bossy, spiteful or serene. Some find it easy to make relationships with the grandchildren — others are more distant. There are also many different ways of showing love and we do not necessarily love people in exactly the same way. Grandparents are not paragons of the family (as Rosemary Wells says in her book *Your Grandchild and*

You) but are humans like everybody else. More will be said about perception in regard to 'sayings' of the grandchildren and in Chapter 5, Towards Understanding.

Mistaken beliefs

Adult children often believe that grandparents are always available. Ann, a young parent, was disappointed when her mother said no to babysitting. 'I don't think she cares about us.' That is not necessarily so, as grandparents have the right to say yes or no. This doesn't mean they are disinterested or not loving. They too have their own lives to lead.

Another myth is, that all grandparents welcome their role. Nothing is further from the truth. What about those in their forties, who, having only just let their own children go, are looking forward to some freedom? They don't want to be tied down. They may also feel grandparenthood puts expectations on them that they are not ready for.

Bonding between grandparents and grandchildren also varies, just as it does in the parent/child relationship, and some people just do not like children.

Grandparents are sometimes considered to be ignorant. The English proverb, 'Don't teach your grandmother to suck eggs' has some meaning. There are certain things that grandparents will know a great deal about and their wisdom and experience can be very useful. Grandparents have to work out their own lives and decide how they want to play the grandparent role. Rose said she was prepared to be a granny, but not a nanny, whereas Joan just longed to take care of the children.

MYTHS FROM GRANDPARENTS

Often grandparents think they know best. Have you met some grandparents who seem to make a career of advising?

They are always right about when to put the baby to bed or when to put a dummy in her mouth — or what the children should do, see, and eat and how to discipline. 'I wouldn't let my child go out at night. The children are overtired — you do too much with them.' They are constantly questioning and undermining the parents. 'Now in my day we stayed at home more!'

The words, 'in my day' often brings horrors to the young. Experience and wisdom can be useful but the old way is not necessarily the best. Here is a story to illustrate this. Esther walked into the kitchen and found her mother roasting a chicken. The mother cut off both the wings. 'Why do you do that?' asked Esther. 'Because my mother did,' the mother answered. Esther asked her grandmother the same question and she answered in the same way. Luckily, Esther could put the same question to her great-grandmother, who said, 'Because the chicken wouldn't fit into the pan. The pan was too small, so I cut off the wings.' Times change and the old ways do not necessarily apply.

FAVOURITES

There is a myth that grandparents will love and treat their grandchildren the same. This is not necessarily true because sometimes we have favourites. Perhaps we have a soft spot for the firstborn, or the child of the daughter we see frequently. Maybe we like a personality which is like our own, or we dislike the traits we see in a child which remind us of the bad side of ourselves. Sometimes, we like girls more than boys, or vice versa.

Perhaps, when there is a divorce, or where there is only one parent, some grandchildren need us more. This does not mean that we are neglectful of the others. Distance makes a relationship harder unless a big effort is put into keeping the contact going. When grandparents in a group were asked whether they had a favourite grandchild, there was much uneasiness and embarrassment. Do we not also favour some friends? Every person is unique and different from anyone else and loves and cares in different ways.

Adult children are sometimes not regarded as capable, and their parenting criticised. There is so much we can learn from our adult children in the way of ideas, values and attitudes. They are also important for their knowledge of what is happening in the modern world. I am indebted to my family for what they have taught me. With grandchildren, it is also a two-way exchange. We can dispel the myth that grandparents don't teach grandchildren and grandchildren don't teach grandparents. Who is the teacher? Who is the pupil?

HOW WE CAN LEARN FROM EACH OTHER

Learning from the grandchildren

• How to have fun and laugh. Having no responsibility — just loving them the way they are.

• How to do new things, like using computers, videos, electrical appliances, and a Walkman. How about the new maths? Ben, aged 8, on showing his grandmother how to use a computer asked, 'How come a 67-year-old knows less than an 8-year-old?' That is hard to answer.

• How to enjoy stories and fairytales again. How many times does Goldilocks have to run away from the three bears?

• For migrants, how to learn English.

• How to feel regenerated and how to explore the modern world.

- How to play games.
- How to feel young again and do crazy things.
- How to collect shells and natural treasures — dried leaves in autumn, seed pods, bark of trees, beach pebbles. One grandmother calls it adventure walks.
- How to surf on a boogie board.
- How to bring out the inner child and re-energise — flying in the backyard as an aeroplane or roaring like a lion.
- How to be re-educated, listening to modern music such as Michael Jackson.
- How to learn new jokes. Ted asked 'Who looks after a haunted house? The answer — a skeleton staff.'

Learning from the grandparents

- How to look at and appreciate nature. Learn the names of trees, flowers and plants. How to learn about birds. The way they live, build nests and migrate.
- How to learn about the olden days. Jack loved to hear about his grandfather's army days.
- How to play games that you can't buy in the shops. Grandfather John had a traditional game where he wrote with his finger on the backs of the children. They were to guess what he was writing.
- How to give cuddles and kisses.
- How to make cup cakes.
- How to have friendship and love.
- How to share memories, photos, letters, old toys and books.
- How to learn about different work places. (As a child, Mike went to watch his grandfather restoring antiques. He also saw his grandmother making her own clothes, using interesting fabrics. Today, Mike has a business incorporat-

ing both those things.)
- How to share thoughts and difficulties — and give lap time for the little ones and a bolt hole for the teenagers.
- How to learn some history.
- How to play cards, knit, play sport and learn hobbies. Jono, aged seven, said old people should do something new, like his grandfather who creates wonderful objects in the carpentry room. Jono thought his grandfather could become famous, like young people who stand on a stage and sing.
- How to enjoy special attention. Try special foods and enjoy treats.
- How to enjoy films, theatre and music. Jim maintained that he got his love of music of the swing era from his grandparents. He wouldn't have had an opportunity to learn about it without their knowledge and records.
- Doing activities parents do not like, for example, fishing, boating, kite flying, horse riding etc.
- Teaching hygiene and manners (not always acceptable).
- How to find a sense of place and identity in the world.
- What it means to be the oldest generation. Children know what it is like to be babies and children, and they see their parents going through the adult stage. Grandparents model the later years.

Adult children and grandparents can share their different worlds and in this way enrich their relationships. Again, the myths need to be dispelled that you can't learn from the young and that you can't teach an old dog new tricks. Growth is possible at any age.

Before we leave myths we need to look at the myth that 'families are meant to be happy'. This is unrealistic. We are all human and there will be both sad and unhappy times in our lives. The conflicts and disappointments are part of life, as well as joys and thrills.

At all times, we have to realise that we are all separate human beings. We do not own our children and grandchildren and we always have to let them go. This excerpt from Kahlil Gibran's *The Prophet* endorses this.

> *Your children are not your children,*
> *They are the sons and daughters of Life's longing for itself*
> *They come through you but not from you.*
> *And though they are with you, yet they belong not to you.*
> *You may give them your love but not your thoughts.*
> *For they have their own thoughts.*
> *You may house their bodies but not their souls,*
> *For their souls dwell in the house of tomorrow,*
> *Which you cannot visit, not even in your dreams.*
> *You may strive to be like them, but seek not to make them like you,*
> *For life goes not backward nor tarries with yesterday.*

REALITIES

Feelings on becoming grandparents

I asked a group of grandparents how they felt on becoming grandparents. Not all of them were full of joy. If you find your new role as a grandparent difficult you are not alone. Out came a whole host of feelings. Mary mentioned how she felt displaced when her grandchild arrived. Seeing her son completely absorbed with his baby and not able to look at her needs brought pangs of jealousy. She had been used to being the centre of attention.

Jane expressed her envy that her daughter had it 'easy'. 'She has all the mod cons — a washing machine, dryer, nappy service, microwave oven, electronic devices. In my day, we were flat out doing everything ourselves.'

Others reported feelings of joy, love and exhilaration. John, on seeing his grandson, was questioning: 'There he is now, but who am I?' Jill at first froze when she got near the baby. She wasn't sure how she felt. It often takes time to get used to a new role. There can also be feelings of fear, anxiety, perplexity and worry, especially for grandparents with very young adult daughters who sometimes have no partners — this can happen in the teenage group. A grandfather described his feelings as catastrophic as he felt it was too soon for his child to become a parent.

People who become grandparents at a young age may not welcome the idea and could regard it as a stigma. This could especially apply to a youthful woman who is not ready for the role. Others see grandparenting as a regeneration and a continuity of their lifeline. With my first grandchild, I remember how my stomach churned and I experienced a multitude of feelings, highlighted by extreme joy and excitement.

Good feelings may come later

Watching children grow, develop and play can be very rewarding and cause an upsurge of warm human emotions. When Joe's grandfather, Max, was recuperating from heart surgery, Joe offered to lend him his prized possession, his Game Boy. Max, who had been a little distant, found it hard to describe the wonderful feelings he had with this offer.

The older generation men often prefer older children and don't take an active part when they are babies. However, it might not be long before they find themselves singing the theme from *Playschool* instead of an operatic aria, or kicking a ball in the backyard rather than playing golf.

Sometimes, living alone brings very little physical contact. Bereaved people have a special feeling of renewal as they hold someone close again and can enjoy the closeness of touching, a wet kiss and a cuddle.

JEALOUSY OF THE PARENTS

How do adult children feel about grandparents? Sometimes they too can be jealous. Jean and Peter said that whenever the grandparents came to visit the grandchildren, they were completely ignored. Even the initial greeting was made to the children. This was in complete contrast to all the attention they had received from the grandparents before. Jean said she only received criticism and felt angry and resentful. Separate outings for the parents and grandparents, without the children, are necessary to cement the relationships and sometimes, not only gifts for the children but also the new parents.

Sometimes parents see the grandparents as more experienced and competent in raising a family. They can feel insecure about this and jealous at the way their children respond and behave with the grandparents. In a way, they feel as if they are the bad guys and the grandparents are the goodies. Then again, grandparents do not experience the nitty-gritty of everyday life with the children — the whingeing, screaming, sulking and so on. They can just close the door and walk away.

Mary was angry that her mother never loved her the way she loves the grandchildren. 'How come you did it all wrong with me? You never spent time with me.'

On the other hand, there is often a great feeling of love and wanting to share all the big moments we go through — a first smile or tooth, all the firsts of clapping hands, crawling, standing, walking, the first day at school and all the other milestones on life's road.

Reality — some slowing down

The reality of growing older can be a lessening of energy and a decline in physical strength. We slow down in certain respects — wrinkles appear, it is time to wear glasses, we puff up the hill, we don't hear so well and we seem to be growing outwards not upwards. Memory can start to play tricks. How often I have searched for my keys and found them in the fridge or in my coat pocket. I didn't notice my glasses were on my nose when I turned the house upside down in search of them.

Like the young, grandparents need affirmation, stimulation, emotional nourishment, a challenge and permission to be themselves. They also need dignity, good medical services, money, useful work and play. It is impossible to be perfect grandparents but it is like a second chance. A sticker on the back of a car in London read, 'I love my grandchildren, I wish I'd had them first'.

Despite the myths, and some slowing down, grandparents play a vital role in community and family life. Figures from the US indicate that 12 per cent of the population are 65 or older, and 70 per cent are grandparents. In Australia, the figure is near 15 per cent and it is expected to rise to 22 per cent by the year 2020. These people are already making an impact in numbers and on the everyday life of the community. Golda Meier of Israel, George Bush of the US and Bob Hawke of Australia, were all leaders and grandparents in their later years. Are they not saying about the indefatigable Margaret Thatcher, the elder statesman, that Granny will be there with her views?

Grandparents have a right and need to live their own lives and cannot expect their grandchildren to satisfy all their dreams and hopes. There is no need to crumble on reaching the grandparenting stage. On the contrary, we need to celebrate having lived to this point and celebrate the things we can do now. Helen Hayes, an actress who died recently at 92, was asked what kept her alive so long. She replied, 'to rest is to rust'.

This confirms medical studies that show that underactivity is a recipe for ill health.

> *As the cells in my body renew,*
> *And my purpose in life I review,*
> *I find growing older*
> *I'm now growing bolder,*
> *And increasingly hard to subdue.*
>
> **Helen G. Ansley**

Grandparents need to continue to educate themselves and learn. At the same time, we have to teach society that older people do not have to be put in a separate box. The minute we are born we start to grow older and we travel along a continuum. The over-sixties and over-eighties are often lumped together even though their problems can be quite different. Have you ever heard of three-year-olds and eight-year-olds being put under the same stage heading? We are all travelling on life's path and have reached different positions. There is a saying, 'Age is all in the mind and usually someone else's'.

There is a lot of work to be done in debunking myths and accepting ageing as something natural and positive. As Betty Friedan says, in her book *Fountain of Age*, 'There is no need to deny ageing, but look at different possibilities.'

This is my grandmother telling me to use a knife and fork to eat a pizza
Andrew (9 yrs)

Grandma and I finishing the castle made from playing cards
William (8 yrs)

CHAPTER 3

Open your ears and close your mouth

*t*he world is sometimes an unfair and difficult place in which to live. Unfortunately, we are unable to prevent our adult children and grandchildren from falling or stumbling along the road of life. However, we can work towards being as supportive and understanding as possible, and in this way we can enrich our relationships. At the same time we can help them to become more mature, take responsibility for themselves and gain more self-esteem.

WHAT DO YOU THINK MAKES A GOOD GRANDPARENT?

I asked a group of grandparents this question. There were many and varied answers. Gillian felt that there was no recipe. You just have to follow your own instincts. Being a good grandparent is really providing a buffer zone. Other comments were, 'I have never really delved into it.' 'I think I have accepted it as an extension of the family.' 'It seems to come naturally.'

Some people thought that time to listen and play was important. Others mentioned involvement without intrusion, love, humour and a tolerance of behavioural differences due to different generational standards.

Eleanor said, 'Support, love — and shutting up. I have to keep on reminding myself that I am not their mother'. One grandfather thought mutual trust, a giving of yourself without seeking anything in return and providing a stable, warm environment were the attributes of a good grandparent. A grandmother maintained that her relationship with her family was good because she allowed her grandchildren to grow in their own ways and did not ask them to fulfill her expectations. She also only gave advice when asked, was there when needed but also was ready to impart any learning from her own experience. In this way, she was an example of what an older person can be like — giving some balance and continuity to life. Val mentioned that she acted silly, behaved like a clown — and enjoyed it. Fun is so important in our lives and laughter is certainly the best medicine.

A great many of the traits mentioned above are to do with good communication. If you can keep the lines open by listening and talking, it is a good start. This chapter will deal with listening — what works well and what doesn't.

BEING DISCOUNTED

Communication can be learnt so that we can say the right word at the right time or even, perhaps, to zip our mouths and say nothing at all. Grandparents have to realise they are human too and it is acceptable to make mistakes.

Apologising when you have done, or said, something that you didn't like is important, as difficult as it may be.

Have you ever met a person who always thinks they are right? How irritating it is. The message that comes through from such people is that we are inferior and don't know very much. We start to doubt ourselves. Have you ever been feeling down and upset, and in need of some comfort? As soon as you mention your troubles, your friend goes one better!

> Mary: I've been sick all week with a bad 'flu. I feel awful and haven't been able to go out for days. It is very depressing.
>
> Joan: Oh, I have such sore ears and last month I was very ill for weeks. I couldn't lift my head. I think I'll go to the doctor today. I feel dreadful.
>
> Mary: (feeling deflated) Oh yes. I'll speak to you another time. Goodbye. (She wasn't going to get any support there.)

Len was in hospital with a sore back and was to have an operation. His wife Joan came in to see him.

> Len: I feel dreadful and worried about the operation.
>
> Joan: Don't be so negative. You're not in Bosnia. You are in a good hospital and have excellent medical attention.
>
> Len: The pain is bad.
>
> Joan: Why don't you look out the window at the beautiful trees and flowers.
>
> Len: I don't want to do that. I want to be up and about. I wish it were all over.

Joan was not sensitive to Len's fears and not accepting of his feelings. Hearing about the ills of the world does not necessarily help the other person as, in times of trouble, they are too absorbed with their own problems.

LISTENING

Listening is one of the hardest skills to acquire. It isn't taught at school — and it doesn't come naturally. It requires putting personal needs and opinions aside at that moment and waiting for someone else to talk. What a luxury it is, in our high-pressure world, to have another person lend an ear and really listen to us. No wonder coffee shops thrive as people let their hair down over cappuccinos. And the pubs are crowded with lonely and isolated people wanting to have a yarn.

The seventies, known as the time of the 'me' generation, produced people who were totally involved in themselves. They had lost interest in others and had to do their own thing. This, of course, can be positive, but only if balanced with caring about what is happening to those around us. In the nineties, there is still evidence that some only care about themselves.

Listening versus hearing

Listening is not the same as hearing. We hear the musak or radio playing in the background while we work, shop and do other things. However, when we listen to a specific piece of music or a lecture we are interested in, we focus on it. Sometimes when we are talking, other people hear us but their thoughts are elsewhere. They are not listening. The message is going in one ear and out the other. How often have you talked to somebody who then gets glassy-eyed, fidgets and seems disinterested?

We older generation of grandparents were taught to always say nice things. We had to be polite even when we were angry and smile when feeling sad. These are contradictory messages and difficult to read. It was also hard to get too close to people when they were not prepared to listen and accept feelings. Hopefully, with adult children and grandchildren we can do something different and listen not just to the words but also to what feelings lie underneath. An ability to listen leads to closeness — and as we have been given two ears and only one mouth, we can listen twice as much as we talk.

During the summer months I was sitting at the poolside of a hotel. Two young children were endeavouring to get their mother's attention.

'Look at me doing handstands underwater', shouted the six-year-old girl.

'Mooom', screamed the older boy, 'I can dive very deep.'

The mother sighed and muttered something to herself. She looked exhausted after eight long weeks of school holidays.

'Just go and play,' she pleaded. 'I don't want to hear anymore from you.'

At that moment, a grey-haired man opened the pool gate and started paying attention, listening to the children's chatter. He had appeared at the right moment and was able to offer time and attention. This was a boon for the parent and some fun for the grandfather. It is very hard for anyone to listen when they feel drained, tired and over-extended. Always explain that you cannot listen when you are worried, or busy, or preoccupied with other things.

Why is it that there is often a wall or barrier between adults and children? There are three different ways that grandparents react to help perpetuate these barriers.

Putting down, lecturing, judging

This example shows a grandfather talking to his adult daughter.

Grandpa John: How are you Janice?
Janice: Not too good. Elly (aged 8) is sick.
John: You shouldn't have let her swim on such a cold day.
Janice: She has a sore stomach and feels bad.
John: Too many lollies and parties. I wouldn't let her stay up so late. Children shouldn't rush around so much. It's bad for them.
Janice: Well I suppose so.
John: Why don't you look after her a bit better? Supervise her diet and keep her at home more?
Janice: Oh, never mind, it doesn't matter.
(Resentment at being told what to do.)

This has been a good piece of demolition work. Janice probably feels stupid and inadequate as a parent.

Patronising, advising

John: How are you Janice?
Janice: Not good. Elly is sick.
John: Oh, you poor thing. I'll call the doctor.
Janice: No don't do that.
John: Why not – you're having a bad time. When you children were sick we stayed with you all day and looked after you. I'll bring some tablets. You know you have to be careful when kids are sick. They can get worse.
Janice: Bye Dad.

Where were the open ears? Janice could get the idea that there was something wrong with her and she certainly must have felt she wasn't as capable as her father.

Distracting

John: How are you Janice?
Janice: Not good. Elly is sick.
John: Oh, she'll be fine. Why don't you come to a film with me? Do you know what is showing up the road?
Janice: I'm worried about her.
John: We could have dinner first and then go out. Elly can just stay in bed. She'll be fine.
Janice: You're not listening to me.

Janice may easily have got the feeling that her father just didn't care about her or her child. He wasn't listening to her and just changed the subject. The real difficulty is not dealt with and the relationship suffers. Feeling brushed aside, Janice might easily take her problems elsewhere next time.

These three examples illustrate how demeaning it can be for the other person and how communication gets blocked and the relationship suffers.

WHAT MAKES A NON-LISTENER?

- Someone who interrupts all the time.
- A person who cuts you off and finishes your sentences. This is a most frustrating experience.
- Sarcasm and making jokes about everything.
- The big interrogator who constantly bombards with questions.

- Those who falsely ass-u-me what the other person means. This makes an ass of you and me and can be quite dangerous.
- Somebody who pretends they are listening but are thinking about other things. Their minds and eyes wander elsewhere.

So what is needed for good communication? Many grandparents are natural communicators so the following is suggested to add to the skills you already have.

Time and inclination

These are important. When people are tired, sick, overloaded or without energy, it is hard to tune in to someone else. It is not a good idea to try to listen under these circumstances. Postpone it until later but make sure you get back to whatever it is. Grandparents often have a great deal of time to offer and are not so emotionally involved as the parents. They also want very much to be with their grandchildren.

Body language

Have you ever had the experience of talking to another person who is standing up and you are sitting down, or vice versa? There is a feeling of distance and being overpowered. You feel a lack of personal involvement. It is also very hard to transmit a message from a different level. I was at a party when the person talking to me kept looking over my head to see who was coming across the room. I froze and immediately stopped talking. I felt completely ignored and reluctant to continue the conversation. How about talking to someone in another room.? You are not able to see facial expressions and the actual word content can get misheard. What happens in households when families try to carry on conversations from one end of a house to the other, or when the bath water is running? In an important communication eye-to-eye level is essential.

Little grandchildren are constantly looking up to adults, so sometimes getting down on creaky knees, close to the floor where they are, helps a great deal. It has been researched that 70 per cent importance is placed on how our bodies look when we send a message, 23 per cent on the tone of voice, and only 7 per cent on what we actually say. This came as quite a surprise to me.

Do we look menacing, attentive, bored, disinterested, or involved? Are we shouting, growling, whispering, mumbling, or talking clearly? What are we saying? Is it appropriate, irrelevant, or not worth hassling about? Do we look sad, but say we are happy? Are we angry but still with a smile on our face? We have to be congruent so that the body language fits the feeling. Observing ourselves listening or getting a message across, can be quite helpful. Avoid lecturing, criticising and scolding. It is also not a good idea to give unasked-for advice.

GUIDELINES FOR LISTENING

- Face each other about 80 centimetres (30 inches) apart.
- Keep eye contact. Be on the same level as the children (down on the carpet) or with adults at their level.
- You must have time and motivation to give full attention. It doesn't work if you are tired, or have hundreds of other things to do at the same moment.
- To listen, keep ears wide open and mouths zipped.

Useful guidelines

Silence – our world is a noisy place. The supermarkets, lifts, roads, hotels and skies are humming. Mobile telephones are ringing incessantly. In Hong Kong, children are virtually electronically wired to their homes to receive messages such as 'Your noodles are ready'. Silence is hard to find and often people feel they have to keep talking when they are with someone as there can be some anxiety lest they do not get in first. Just being quiet can bring out a great deal in another person and also shows interest and concern. It is a powerful message of acceptance and indicates that you are ready to listen. This is especially useful when a member of the family, or a friend, has a problem and feels sad, angry or frightened. It is difficult not to jump in, boots and all, and have your say but that is not very effective.

Acknowledgements: it is useful to nod, say Hmm', Yes', Uh-huh', Really', to indicate you have heard what has been said. It also indicates you are tuned in to the other person and will be offering no judgement.

Door-Openers are open-ended invitations to the other person to say some more. It requires more than a Yes' or No' answer. For example, Would you like to tell me about it?' Can you say a little more?' Sounds like you have a lot of feelings about that.' It is non-threatening and encourages the other person to continue talking. These three guidelines are helpful but are limited in effectiveness and lead onto Active Listening.

Adults and children blossom when they have a one/one relationship and they can have undivided attention. A tall order but it works. I have noticed how much my family thrives when they are seen alone. There is such a diversity of interests and needs that when everyone is together there can be little individual attention. It takes much more time, especially when there are 17 family members, but it is worth it.

So the barriers and walls are up when we do all the talking, provide the solutions and take away self-responsibility. They come down when we listen.

Active listening

Active listening and its principles comes from Thomas Gordon's books on Parent Effectiveness. However, we can equally apply this skill to grandparenting and in fact any relationship.

Let's look at the example of John and Janice using Active Listening.

> John: How are you Janice?
> Janice: Not good Elly is sick.
> John: You must be worried (tuning in to her feelings).
> Janice: Yes I am. She has a high temperature so I called the doctor.
> John: It is very difficult when kids get sick. It also disrupts the household and creates more work.
> Janice: Yes, I was supposed to go in to my job today. I'm worried about missing the pay.
> John: It's hard to balance home and work especially when someone is not well.
> Janice: Yes, I am also getting tired and edgy.
> John: What do you think you will do?
> Janice: I don't really know. Perhaps make up the hours on another day.
> John: Can I help you in any way?
> Janice: Thanks. Can you fetch Anna from school then I won't have to drag Elly out?

In this example John really listened. He showed a great

deal of empathy and tried to put himself in Janice's shoes as to what she was feeling. He put his own needs aside and attended to hers. He also offered practical help which can be very welcome. The relationship between them was warm and loving. Active Listening is listening carefully, feeding back both verbally and non-verbally, with empathy and warmth, the speaker's message. In this way others can get rid of troublesome feelings and be understood. It is a way of getting close and having good relationships without the other person feeling inhibited and put down.

The main criteria for helping and supporting others are Active Listening, attending, accepting.

What will help

- Spend time and really listen.
- Encourage expression of feelings.
- Be empathic (feeling with somebody).
- Give hugs and kisses where appropriate.
- Let grandchildren and adult children solve their own problems.
- Accept them as people with their own ideas.

What won't help

- Doing other things and trying to listen at the same time.
- Lecturing and judging. Saying how it should be.
- Putting on the spot with lots of questions like in a courtroom. A boy of eight said he was teaching his grandmother to listen by telling her not to ask so many questions, and not listening to her when she did.
- Reassuring – it doesn't help to say everything will be fine tomorrow when someone is in the middle of difficulties.
- Do everything for them – take away their ability to solve their own problems.

- Brush off their feelings.
- Push someone to talk when they don't want to.

Young children are often not sure of their feelings and they are undifferentiated. They do not exactly know what they are experiencing so feeding back the feeling could be quite difficult. What usually can be picked up is whether they are feeling glad, sad, or mad. These feelings don't last very long and they can run off and play or change the subject very quickly. Sometimes they hide feelings and act them out in different ways. Pulling the dog's tail, pinching their brother or sister, withdrawing or refusing to eat can be signs that something is wrong. If they are not being listened to there is a strong need to try and get attention in some other way.

Listening is a skill that takes time and practice to acquire. In Australia, classes for Parent Effectiveness (Thomas Gordon) are held around the country. Perhaps there could be one for grandparents to sharpen up some of the skills that they probably have already, like the grandparenting groups run by the Tresillian Family Care Centres

The hardest thing that I have found is to have a degree of separation between family and myself. I remember when I went to see my mother as a grown woman of 55. She was still holding my jacket and telling me to put it on because I'd catch cold. Separating is necessary for survival in a world of constant happenings. It is easy to get emotionally immobilised by what we hear. We may not like it and not be able to listen. It is not pleasant to encounter sadness, disappointment and anger and we often want to avoid the issue. Grandparents don't have to keep their children and adult children happy and solve their problems. Taking a step back can be a help. They can just be there to support with love, honesty and empathy so that families can grow and cope with the world.

Grandparenthood gives us a second chance of relating to families. We must recognise each other's needs and feelings and realise each person has the right to run their own lives and make mistakes. That is often a good way of learning. Even young children can take some self-responsibility and find their own ways.

I do not want to minimise the wisdom of the elders and the huge amount of folklore and history that is passed down from one generation to another. However, there is a time and place for it and it must be given when wanted and not enforced on others.

Having grandchildren can be a joyous experience but it can be tinged with sorrow, sickness and difficulties. It is perhaps a reflection of the world and the reality of life. Just being there and listening can be a great help and in this way the relationship can be enriched. If we listen to our grandchildren and adult children we have a good chance of them listening to us and getting closer. We can also begin to look at things in different ways, not just our way, and this can lead to a great deal of self-discovery. By becoming aware of the feelings, attitudes and needs of others we can, at the same time, become aware of these things in ourselves.

Apart from listening just to others we can tune in to the sounds around us. The singing of the birds, the roaring of the waves, the rustling of the grass and so much else that nature offers. We can pay more attention to our favourite music and above all the joyful sounds of children chattering and laughing as they play.

So far we have been looking at the needs of others and how to listen to them. You may well be thinking by now who is going to listen to you? In the next chapter I will deal with unzipping the mouth in order to share those pearly bits of wisdom and experience. Grandparents will also have a chance of seeing how to assert themselves so that there is less danger of exploitation and being reduced to a 'doormat.'

Your ears must be feeling over-worked and worn out. What about the mouth? It probably is uncomfortable from holding back all the words you had in mind to say. Listening is not easy to do and sometimes feels artificial. However, it is certainly worth the effort as American writer Lois Wyse says, Grandchildren are the dots that connect the line from generation to generation'.

Hearing someone out without judging can lead to enriched relationships, not only with family but also with friends. Now there needs to be an opportunity for you to have your say in order to get a balance between your needs and those of others.

*Grandpa on Mum's side.
He was an artist.*

Jessie (8 yrs)

CHAPTER 4
THE ASSERTIVE GRANDPARENT

Do not go gentle into that good night,
Old age should burn and rage at close of day,
Rage and rage at the dying of the light.
Dylan Thomas

Many people who are now grandparents were brought up to believe in the puritanical ethic that giving yourself pleasure or looking after your own needs is selfish. If, by chance, you do follow your own needs, a huge amount of guilt rests on your shoulders. You were taught to be polite and to say nice things. Negative emotions were to be controlled and you never spoke up for yourself — it was too embarrassing. Ken, a grandfather in one of the groups, said that when he was at school he was told not to use the letter 'I' in an essay, only 'one' or 'we'. It is often difficult to change this deprecating programming, but anything learnt can be unlearnt. If grandparents do not look after their own needs it is hard to look after others and feel good about it. Agreeing to cancel appointments in order to help others grudgingly usually doesn't work as the feeling we are left with is one of resentment.

How often have you heard doctors ask a patient, 'How are we today?' Advice is often given as one should do this, or one should do that. For some, 'I' is uncomfortable and denotes an ego trip. Grandparents often think that their attributes are only to be used to please other people. A balance is very necessary in attending to ourselves — this can mean saying no when appropriate, as well as looking after the needs of others.

To start off, I would like to introduce some 'no-no' words.

Say 'I', not 'we' or 'one'. You cannot speak for someone else so it is a good idea to practise saying 'I', even though it may feel uncomfortable at first.

Don't say ought, should or must. These three words have a moralistic flavour and really mean I do not particularly want to do something but am pushing myself along.

Say I won't instead of I can't. The former acknowledges that you take responsibility for your decision not to do something. The latter is cowardly and acknowledges you have no choice. In life, we have choices as to how we live and behave, even in adversity.

Instead of saying always, say sometimes. Always means all the time, which is not possible.

Instead of saying I'll try, say I'll do it. The latter is a positive statement and says you will get on with something to the best of your ability.

FEELINGS AND EMOTIONS

In our world, nobody can be happy all the time. We have any number of feelings about everyday happenings and they can be divided into two types — pain or pleasure. The older generation of grandparents was reared at a time when it was frowned upon to express feelings. A stiff upper lip was the order of the day for most Anglo-Saxons.

Emotions, as distinct from thoughts (head stuff), are bodily sensations that we feel in different degrees in response to someone or something. If not expressed in a healthy way, they can gnaw at the very roots of family relationships and, in the end, destroy them. There are four basic emotions — anger, fear, sadness and joy. Many other feelings evolve from these four, such as jealousy, guilt, anxiety, excitement, helplessness and happiness.

Anger is very much part of our lives. It can erupt and be destructive, or constructive when we can use words to stand up for ourselves so that we do not get exploited. (Exploitation is common in our ageing society where the old are considered powerless.)

Have you seen people who smile when they are annoyed? They talk as if they are not angry but their body language is a give-away. Muscles tighten, their skin goes red, breathing stops, and they can look as though they are bursting. Whatever does it do to their insides? Feelings are transitory and, if expressed, can disappear.

Fear keeps us away from danger, but it also prevents us from taking risks, visiting new places and doing things we haven't done before. We usually feel fear when we lose something (it could be about losing face) or are deprived in some way.

Sadness helps us to express our losses. Crying can

have a cleansing and releasing effect. Some people find this very difficult, particularly older men, as it was thought very weak to cry. Hopefully, it is now more acceptable.

Joy – being able to express negative feelings helps to find the positives underneath. Life can then be enjoyed with lots of pleasures and satisfactions. (For more on this, see Chapter 8, Enrichment.)

It is not uncommon to experience mixed feelings about the same things. For example, Josh was very excited over the birth of his new grandchild but he also felt apprehensive as to what role he was to play.

COPING WITH POWER AND DEMANDS

Are you the sort of person who finds it hard to say no, but feels resentful when you say yes? So often, grandparents agree to requests from adult children which they would rather not do. Esther, a grandmother of three small grandchildren, came back from her holiday saying how wonderful it was to be doing something for herself and not feel tugged in so many directions. Martin had to tell his daughter he was not available for babysitting as he was coming to the grandparenting group meeting. In the past, he would either have said yes and felt resentful, or said no and carried a great deal of guilt. This is not to imply that saying yes is not important, but it should not be at an emotional cost.

Let us look at how most people cope when faced with demands, or when pressure is inflicted upon them.

Usual Ways of Coping
Flight
Retreat, withdraw physically

psychologically

Fight
Hitting back
Aggression
Wars and quarrels

Submit
Give in
Conform

Alternative Ways of Coping

Flight
Stand your ground, listen
Take a risk

Fight
Confront
Be assertive
'I' messages

Submit
Is it worth the hassle?
Do I need it?
Listen and 'I' messages.

Flight

So many people use flight in desperation, to get away from the conflict. It is much easier to avoid issues but doesn't usually solve anything. When a situation is difficult, grandparents often withdraw to community groups, or stay away and avoid their families. The same applies to adult children in a situation where there are constant hassles. They stop seeing parents on a regular basis and regard visits as a chore rather than a pleasure. In this way, the relationship suffers. Grandparents can be very passive and say very little when something annoys them; alternatively, they will grin and bear it, as in the Victorian era. This kind of silence can be very hurtful to the other person. As well, repressed negative feelings can cause physical ailments such as ulcers, migraines, nausea and various aches and pains. Later, a person can also explode because of pent-up feelings and a great deal of damage can be done.

Fight or aggression

Aggressive grandparents are angry with their adult children a great deal of the time. It could be a carry-over from childhood days, a jealousy of their youth and lifestyle, or a feeling of not being considered or cared for. A great deal of yelling, put-downs and sarcasm can result. 'I never see the children.' 'You are always too busy to think about me.' 'You're selfish and thoughtless.' How many times do we hear such nagging and similar conversations using the no-no words. The aggression can be hurtful and do harm. Adult children become rebellious and the relationship deteriorates.

Submit

How many grandparents say yes to all requests and then feel resentful at not being able to live their own lives? Grandmother Pearl accepted an invitation to go to a friend's house for dinner in two weeks time. On the day of the outing, her daughter rang and said she needed a babysitter as she had a meeting. Pearl agreed to look after the children, but underneath she was very disappointed at not being able to meet her own needs, and she felt she had little control over her life. Submitters usually do what is demanded of them but, in the process, deny their own needs and values. Grandparents can find their time monopolised by child-minding, doing the shopping, chauffeuring, caring for the sick, and other jobs. This is acceptable only if it is convenient and feels right for you.

There are more productive ways of coping, although it is often a balancing act between looking after the needs of others and attending to ourselves. It is hard to know when to hold our tongues and when to speak up.

Assertive

Being assertive, rather than aggressive or passive, is important. The latter can mean the other person can get their needs met at your expense and aggression can be that you are getting your needs met at the expense of the other person. For example, Mary, when asked to fetch her grandchild from school, shouted and screamed, 'You should have told me earlier. You are very thoughtless as I also have things to do and I have my own life to lead. I'm not your slave'. That illustrates an aggressive reaction. A submissive reaction would be, 'Yes, I'll fetch today. I was going to the pictures — but I will put my arrangements off. They are not important'.

WHAT SORT OF GRANDPARENT ARE YOU?

Soft Grandparents

- I have to please everyone so I must say yes.
- My needs are not important.
- The needs of adult children, grandchildren and others are more important than mine.
- I can't say no without feeling guilty.

Firm Grandparents

- I can say no without feeling guilty.

- My needs are as important as those of others.
- I have my own life to lead.
- I am human and will have to let others know what I choose to do.

So how is it possible to be assertive and enrich our relationships? An assertive person is clear, firm and direct. We need to empower ourselves and show how we want to be treated. In the US, Grey Power has resulted in radical changes to legislation.

Let's look at what Mary could have said to her daughter. 'I made my arrangements two weeks ago and will not be able to fetch from school today. With some notice, I would be happy to do so another time.'

Using an 'I' message means revealing some part of ourselves. It takes courage to say what you think and feel but it also sets the path for others to be open and honest with us. Mary's daughter may not have liked the outcome, but she won't feel guilty about asking her mother another time as she knows she will be up-front with her. A suggested structure for 'I' messages could be the following. Not all three steps have to be used and the order can be changed. Once again, the concept comes from Thomas Gordon's book, *Parent Effectiveness Training*.

'I' MESSAGE

- Describe the other person's behaviour or request.
- What is your feeling?
- What effect does it have on your time, money or energy?

Here is an example of the three steps regarding the subject of punctuality. Jean and Esther made an arrangement to meet for coffee. Jean was constantly 20 minutes late for their meetings and Esther was beginning to boil with rage.

She decided to confront her friend with an 'I' message as the friendship was important to her.

    Esther: When I sit here waiting for you, I feel impatient and resentful as it takes up a lot of my time and I am unable to do other things.
    Jean: I am sorry, I didn't know you felt that way.
    Esther: This has happened so often before. I am getting a bit tired.
    Jean: I'm glad you mentioned it. I'll try to be more punctual.

You have a better chance of salvaging the relationship in this way. If Jean had been defensive and answered, 'I don't care,' Esther might ask herself what she is doing in that friendship. If Esther had not brought it up, she would have been resentful.

Jim drew a picture of how he saw himself in the family. It was a drawing of a hamburger and he was in the middle — a most uncomfortable position. On one side, he had his children and grandchildren, and on the other, his aged mother. It was hard to see where he was squashed in the filling. Jim needed to balance his needs as well as the needs of those around him. It is unpleasant to feel overloaded. People who have sick family members or frail parents to look after are very vulnerable to this situation. The Carers' Association is very helpful in handling these situations and giving carers a break.

Being assertive simply means that you realise you count as a person and that, as other people have rights, so do you. It also requires some communication with ourselves before we speak. I often have long conversations with myself, which helps me to sort out feelings and also to work out what I want to say. Sometimes I will decide the issue is not worth hassling about. At other times, I will rehearse what I intend to say to another person. Communicating with oneself is the first step towards communicating with others. An 'Assertive Bill of Rights' is a helpful reminder that we have to look after ourselves as well as others.

ASSERTIVE BILL OF RIGHTS

I have the right to:
- Be my own final judge.
- Not justify my behaviour to others.
- Refuse to solve other's problems — I can help and support if asked.
- Change my mind.
- Make mistakes and be responsible for the consequences.
- Say 'I don't know'.
- Be independent of other's goodwill.
- Be illogical.
- Say 'I don't understand'.
- Say 'I don't care', (even if people don't like me or criticise me).

It is not much fun being a doormat, being exploited and receiving all the kicks. A relationship is enriched when people are honest and able to reveal themselves. This is not so easy and may mean you take the risk of someone not liking you or your ideas. In the long run, however, it makes for closer relationships and greater self-esteem. Being assertive also gives children permission to be the same. Eileen mentioned how she took her grandson, age 11, to the cinema. He told her he was embarrassed sitting next to her as his friends were sitting three rows behind and he wanted to join them. The relationship remained intact because of the honesty of the grandson and Eileen's acceptance that he needed to show his independence.

Grandparents can share their beliefs and values even if they are different from the points of view of the young. Liv Ullman, after making the film *Sophie*, expressed how important the old values and rituals are. Perhaps there needs to be more sharing of the past without forcing it on anybody. It is also important to disclose positive 'I' messages whenever possible. Some people are very stingy about this, not having received many themselves. It means disclosing how others bring pleasing warmth and joy. No good/bad evaluation is necessary. Some examples of these could be:

- I like the colours of your picture.
- I like the way you laugh:
- I like being with you. I value you as a friend.
- I appreciate your help.
- I like the way you work.
- I enjoy coming to your house.
- Your dress is very pretty.
- I love you.

We are very quick to talk about the negative things, but often take the positives for granted. As plants need water, we need nourishing by sharing the good things. Otherwise, we too may wither and die. Life is a balancing act between co-operating with others and looking after ourselves. Sometimes our needs and those of others can come into conflict.

CONFLICT

Conflict is very much a part of everyday life. It occurs in all families and is connected to the differing needs of family members.

Through the years, most of us have been handling conflicts either in a very strict or authoritarian way, or in a more lenient or permissive manner. The latter method was used particularly after World War 11, when children ruled supreme. Have you ever visited homes where the younger generation has completely taken over? Things are chaotic and you can't get a word in. This often results in resentment from parents and grandparents, who feel they are losing out. Pat, 40, who was brought up in a laissez-faire household, doesn't like it when she watches her children behaving the same way as she did. She now veers more to the other side.

Then there are the households where the parents and grandparents are the bosses and the children feel powerless. Our grandparenting style is often handed down from one generation to another and is made up of our own experiences. To enrich relationships and add to your skills, look at the democratic way.

Being democratic, listening to others but, at the same time, considering yourself and negotiating, makes for mutual understanding. Mediation and conflict resolution is being widely used in the community and business world in order to settle disputes which could get very nasty in the law courts.

DEMOCRACY — HOW DO WE USE IT?

We need to open our ears wide and listen to the other person's point of view and needs. At the same time, we have to look after ourselves and be an assertive grandparent without being harmful to others. As an example, Grandpa Jim was taking his grandson Daniel, 8, out for a treat in the school holidays. He didn't want anything too hectic as he had a sore back. Daniel had his own ideas.

Daniel: I want to go rollerblading.

That was too strenuous for Jim and he felt ill-equipped to deal with that activity.

Jim: (Shuddering) Sorry, that's too much for me to watch and handle. What about the park?
Daniel: No, there is nothing to do there. It's just too boring.
Jim: Give me some other ideas.
Daniel: What about a movie?
Jim: OK, that's fine.

Both agreed, and neither felt they had lost out. They respected each other's needs and came to a mutual decision.

There is a great sense of self-esteem in maintaining a balance between looking after ourselves and, at the same time, considering others. We have a choice in what we do. Sometimes there is a conflict between obligations and our needs and wants. However, we need to have a high regard for ourselves in order to maintain our own health and sense of fulfilment. At the same time, we have to respect others. Perhaps we would have fewer wars if we looked at issues in a different way.

Rabbi Hillel said in the *Talmud*, a Jewish book of law and legend, said:

> *If I am not for myself,*
> *Who will be for me?*
> *If I am for myself alone*
> *What am I?*
> *If not now*
> *When?*

Human like everyone else — they are having a row.

Neil (8 yrs)

CHAPTER 5
*t*OWARDS UNDERSTANDING

*b*eing a parent and a grandparent in today's world can sometimes be a perplexing and bewildering experience. Times have changed considerably since our children were small and it seems that today's babies are almost ready for university enrolment. They attend playgroups, massage and kindygym, and are read quite complex books.

We have to change our thinking to encompass all the changes but, at the same time, it is often a help to know what to expect from children at different ages and stages (keeping in mind that every child is an individual). We can then have some clue as to how to cope and react. It is always a good idea to know what to do when grandchildren come to visit.

Changing the Environment

Before outlining the stages, it is important to realise that, especially with small children, a safe house with at least one childproof room prevents a lot of hassles. How clearly I remember visiting with my twin babies and having anxiety attacks about smashing precious ornaments or spilling orange juice on a pure white carpet. Dangers lurked everywhere — sharp table edges, power points, toppling lamps and safety pins (certainly a misnomer). What's safe?

Quite a few grandparents describe grandchildren's visits as catastrophic. They leave a trail of mess and disorder. Crawling babies and toddlers attack chair covers, electrical points or find a way into dangerous cupboards. They stuff everything available into their gaping mouths. The day is wrought with anxiety and you need to have nerves of steel. Needless to say, when they depart it looks as though a bomb has struck and hours are spent in getting things back in order.

HINTS FOR KEEPING SANITY DURING VISITS

Discuss at the beginning of the visit what rooms are off limits and the rules of the grandparent's house. Lily felt the children needed to wash their hands before meals. This wasn't what they did at home but discussing it with them made them realise that this is what you do at Gran's place.

Keep a space where it doesn't matter if anything happens to the furniture, drapes or carpets. Store any treasures. Make it as safe as possible — keep poisons, pills and sharp kitchen knives well out of reach. Have a special toy box with activities that will interest the grandchildren and a bookshelf with some suitable books.

Safety check

1. Put away all breakable and valuable articles.
2. Pills and medicines must be kept out of reach in locked cupboards.
3. Poisons and household cleaners need to be kept away from little hands.
4. Make electric sockets safe.
5. When cooking, turn pot handles inwards.
6. If possible, use an eye-level oven.
7. Check no small beads, peas, nuts, or sharp articles are lying around.
8. Keep all electric leads and flexes away from crawling babies.
9. Beware of tablecloths dangling over tables.
10. Make sure that no sharp garden tools are lying around.

Using this safety check could eliminate a great deal of anxiety and the potential for torrents of tears.

Inexpensive activities

Older children may need somewhere to run, play their games and work off some steam. A garden is ideal if you have one. Bats and balls are invaluable — as are skipping ropes. In small areas, such as flats, introduce something to keep them busy — it doesn't have to cost much. Waste materials, such as boxes, corks, ribbons, carton tops and boxes, string, plastic bottles, tinfoil and cardboard can keep even the most sophisticated grandchildren very busy. Colouring in, using butcher or computer paper, and cut-outs on coloured scraps can help to fill in the hours. That awful cry 'I'm bored!', has to be avoided at all costs.

Grandparents find, that after a while, they run out of ideas and time may start to hang heavily. Their homes are not necessarily geared to the needs of small children. Looking around the house can inspire some games without toys. Cat's Cradle, a game played with a piece of looped string, has been a special favourite in our family through the generations. It was brought to England as long ago as 1782 and probably originated in Asia. Hiding things and having treasure hunts, playing shadows on the wall, and having a sing-song help to while away the time. What about sound and rhythm games, using pots, pans and wooden spoons — if your ears can stand it! Pen and paper games like noughts and crosses, battleships, hangman, dot-to-dot, are useful. Baking, cooking, carpentry and gardening are fulfilling activities which can be done together. And what about the perennial 'I spy'? See how long you can keep all this going before the grandchildren drift towards the television.

Some recipes of family favourites

Granny Flo's Famous Cup Cakes

This recipe is still in the old measurements, having been handed down through three generations.

$1/4$ lb butter;	5 oz sugar;
$1/4$ teaspoon salt;	1 $3/4$ cups flour;
2 eggs;	2 teaspoons baking powder;
$1/3$ cup milk, or more;	Flavouring optional.

This recipe makes 18 cakes.

Cream sugar and butter. Add eggs, flour and milk alternately. Lastly, add baking powder. Put mixture into paper cases in patty pans and bake at 420 degrees for 10-15 minutes. Ice and decorate when cold.

This is a popular activity for both boys and girls and can be lots of fun. Never mind if the icing ends up on the ceiling or the hundreds and thousands are crushed underfoot.

Chocolate Crispies

This recipe was taken from a Kelloggs' cereal box. Very quick and easy to make and messy to eat.

A bar of cooking chocolate and some cornflakes or rice crispies is all that is needed. Quantities vary according to how many you want.

Melt the chocolate over a pot of hot water, or in the microwave oven. Remove and mix with cornflakes until they are completely covered with chocolate. Set out paper cases on a tray and put a teaspoonful of the mixture into each one. Leave to set for a few minutes. They can go into the refrigerator if they are not gobbled up straight away.

Playdough

This is a non-eating recipe but it is great for moulding and making things.

>   *1 cup of flour, mixed with a cup of salt;*
>   *2 tablespoons of vegetable oil;*
>   *food colouring (optional);*
>   *½ cup of water;*
>   *1 teaspoon of glycerine to keep it moist for longer.*

Mix the ingredients together until a dough is formed. Store the dough in a plastic tub in the fridge. When shaped, the dough can be baked in a cool oven and painted with poster paints.

This can keep grandchildren occupied for some hours and is quite creative. They often welcome time away from their familiar, and sometimes expensive, toys.

Potato Printing

Use good-sized potatoes cut in half. Carve out animal shapes or flower shapes. Dip into paint and press the potato shape onto the paper.

Dressing up Box
Don't give away your old clothes. They can be used for lots of imaginative play. Hats can change personalities. Shoes, shirts, skirts and trousers can take children into other worlds. Pieces of brightly coloured materials, shawls and scarves give surprisingly interesting effects. What about an old white sheet for all those ghosts? If any articles have a sentimental value the past can be brought to life. My wedding veil provides a lot of discussion and imaginative acting.

AN ADULT WORLD

Our world is really designed for adults. Look at the furniture, height of shelves, door knobs, toilets and taps. Try to simplify your home and make it easier for the young — bring yourself down to their level.

Very often grandchildren visit with their parents. The adults begin talking and the grandchildren are left to amble off and may feel neglected. It isn't easy to balance paying attention to parents and grandchildren at the same time, but being aware of this and allocating time can be helpful. At the end of the day, don't be left with the house in a mess — make it a combined effort to clear up together.

Understanding what to expect from grandchildren at their different ages and stages can be very useful.

Ages and Stages

0-6 months
At this stage a baby wants to be safe and secure. All their needs have to be met by others so they learn to trust. Parents are usually very tired looking after a baby and experiencing sleepless nights. A grandparent can be invaluable by taking the baby for a short while — perhaps pushing the pram, looking at nature's mobiles, the swaying

of the trees, the rolling of the waves, watching the birds in flight. Many Africans have a wonderful knack of carrying babies on their backs and continuing their activities. We haven't quite mastered that but the modern papoose is a useful substitute. I recall a picture of a baby being fed by the mother while the father stood behind and massaged the mother's shoulders and a grandparent stood behind and massaged the father. The nurturer has to be nurtured. Parenting the parent, giving support and looking after their needs is vital. Young babies have a knack of drying up all the energy.

It is a jolt when a baby comes into a household and experienced grandparents can be a threat to adult children who are in the beginning unsure of their parenting. Jealousy can rear its head on both sides and diplomacy is needed in not taking the resistance too personally. Bert said when his grandchild was born he wasn't allowed to pick her up for the first three months. Young parents sometimes need to feel their way and develop their parenting identity. Many grandparents may feel ousted when the new baby arrives and want to play a bigger part. It often takes time for everyone to adjust.

6-18 months

At this stage, children need to explore. They touch, smell, watch, chew, bite, taste, hold and drop everything. How difficult it is when toys and food are picked up and flung around the room. It is vital to baby proof the living areas to prevent accidents. I recall a childhood friend's daughter swallowing a necklace. There were numerous trips to the toilet before it came out the other end — luckily. Children of this age have little control — distracting works better than admonishing. This age can be draining for parents and grandparents. Running around after crawlers and early walkers can be very strenuous. Let them make a mess and lower the expectations for a clean house and any sort of orderliness. Some grandparents love this age as they feel needed. Others simply find it exhausting.

18 months - 3 years
At this stage, children want their own way in order to develop a sense of identity. 'No' is often the main, and perhaps only, word in their vocabulary, and yet they are very unsure of what they want. 'I want an apple' they might say, and when they get it they fling it away. A two-year-old can have violent shifts of mood and will bite, kick, bang, and even hold his, or her, breath. It is not called the terrible twos for nothing. They are averse to change and moving from one activity to another can be difficult. To minimise the strain, preparation or advance warning is helpful. 'When you have finished your drawing of the tree we will have lunch.' In their efforts to separate from parents, two-year-olds may cling and hide. They have a mixture of feelings, with little means of communication, and can be exasperating. Some firmness is needed as well as support and love. Baby-sitting is certainly not sedentary but more on the run.

3-6 years
Children move from parallel play to sharing with others, although at kindergarten you still see rows of children playing independently. They have to feel secure before being able to give to others. It is a time for grandparents to tell and read stories and to share secrets. Listening is important — without using any killer statements such as, 'You're naughty, crazy, silly, stupid'. Tune in to their needs, at the same time being firm. It is a time of questioning — what,

how, why and when — which require simple honest answers.

At this age, children want to be big and important and yet physically they are midgets in a world of giants. They can be very imaginative and have imaginary friends and be attached to different toys. They often mimic adults in the home and out in the world. Joan, 4, plays in the toy kitchen. She is constantly pressing buttons and pretending she is using a microwave. Ted and John, aged 5, are running a shop with counterfeit bankcards, and another group of children is making a puppet show. Grandparents can use waste materials (as mentioned under Environment) to keep them busy. At this stage, children become aware of outside dangers and the vulnerability of their bodies. A huge supply of band-aids is a necessity.

6-12 years

Children at these ages are interested mainly in their peers and sometimes ignore grandparents. They often do not want to be kissed and need privacy in the bathroom. Their taste in stories and films has changed. No more *Peter Rabbit,* or *Bambi,* but more likely *Treasure Island* and *Jurassic Park.*

They are beginning to move away from their families. On the other hand, as big as they are, they may still want lap time and cuddles. Their peers and adults are important models and some form of reasoning begins. They often cruise through school and need someone at home at the end of the day to feed, water and love them. They relate to the give and take of the world and are often quite amenable. The diary for the week is crammed with activities such as cricket, dancing, music, soccer, tennis, gym, swimming, hockey and computer lessons. It is understandable that parents and grandparents sometimes feel like taxi drivers.

12-18 years
It has been said that teenagers vacillate between being a pain and a heart melter.

Hormones are flying around — they are neither children, nor adults. On the one hand, they want independence, on the other they crave nurturing. They are an enigma. The physical changes do not necessarily parallel the mental and they seem all over the place. They are often allergic to dressing in time for school, washing and cleaning. They vacillate over making decisions. They are addicted to rock music, junk food, talking on the phone, watching television and looking in the mirror. They are totally disinterested in adults, ego-centred and are never wrong. This can be a trying time — you need a great deal of patience while they 'find' themselves.

Grandparents can try to accept modern music and different ideas. They can participate actively or be spectators clapping madly on the sports field. Accept their friends, even if they seem outrageous, and be there with support when needed. There is no reason to change your values, or to act and dress like teenagers, but there is a great need for the acceptance of differences. Grandchildren can have unusual (to us) thoughts, feelings and activities but caring, respect, a hug, a smile and a sense of humour can accomplish a great deal. Just hanging in there is a help. And it is comforting, as one grandmother said, that they eventually come back as adults and the relationship becomes close again.

Points in this section have been taken from *Your Child's Self Esteem* by Dorothy Corkille Briggs.

LIFE COURSE OF GRANDPARENTING
As grandchildren progress through the years, there are

resulting changes for grandparents, as well as individual likes and dislikes. Some grandparents do not like babies. Others are cuddlers and can't get enough of the first few months. There are men, in particular, who tend to leave infants to the grandmother. Grandfather Max maintained that he could not relate to a child until she or he responded and talked. Jim also mentioned that he only liked his grandchildren when they were grown up. Mike admitted he wasn't a hands-on grandpa. He didn't really know where to start, but he was looking forward to learning.

Mostly, young children can be a source of delight to most grandparents. Childhood is a time for hugging, bouncing on the knee, playing fun games and reading stories over and over again. On the practical side, as babies and toddlers are dependent, grandparents are needed in so many ways — babysitting, driving, playing, and general help in the home. A lot of time, energy and emotions are invested in the early years. It is interesting to see that in many photo albums, most pictures are taken of the first few years and the pre-adolescent period. This can indicate the big part that grandparents play in the early years and the close association they have.

As the children grow older, the relationship can change. The 6 to 12s are busy with friends and seem to have less time for grandparents. However, they are often intrigued with stories of the old times and are ready for treats and outings. Mae said her grandchildren often asked, 'Nana, give us a story from your head'.

The teenagers begin to grow away from the family, searching for their own identities. Grandparents are not needed as much but they can still provide support and a bolt hole — or dinner together and a talk, without the emotional involvement of a parent. A one-to-one relationship can work wonders. Grandparents have to go through another separation as the grandchildren get older, and it isn't always easy to let go again. There can be a distinct feeling of loss. It is important not to feel rejected at this stage — it is a time of growth and development and not a personal rejection. If it seems there is a lack of appreciation it does not mean there won't be appreciation in the future.

Coming back as young adults, there can be a reversal in roles as help is given to grandparents in many ways — helping with the computer, cleaning, gardening and carrying the shopping. Mary, whose husband had died, often received visits from her grandchildren in her holiday house. They went to the beach together and had long walks and talks. When the grandchildren became parents, the lifecycle started all over again for her as a great-grandmother.

The role of grandparenting changes with the ages and stages of the grandchildren. It is a bit like a career that fluctuates as the years pass. It becomes an adult to adult relationship.

WHAT GRANDPARENTS ARE CALLED

Grandparents often spend a lot of time with grandchildren and build close relationships. Thus the names they are given appear to denote affection. They are called Pop, Poppy, Gaga, Gran, Gan, Gramp, Nana, Old Pa or Ma, Grand-dad, Moo, Boo, Grandpa, and Fluft. What a range of names the grandchildren bring forth. My 18-month-old grandson calls me Grabby! I only hope it is because he cannot pronounce his 'n' s. The modern idea of calling grandparents by their Christian names works well for some people, especially when there are two grandparents on each side. However, Ken, aged seven, wanted everyone at school to know he had grandparents so he chose not to use first names. There are also many derivatives of Christian names in use. Grandfather Alexander was called 'Ackie' as it was too much of a mouthful to pronounce in the early days — as was 'Siddy' for Sydney. Children have a knack of finding words.

HOW GRANDCHILDREN REGARD US

Children perceive us in interesting ways. I talked with a number of them and some fascinating thoughts came out. One boy of seven said grandparents are lucky — they have all the time in the world. They can eat when they like, sleep when they like and go out when they please. I detected a sense of envy. Joshua asked why grandparents grow out not up. Amy said her grandfather didn't talk much, he was always reading mystery books and asking her to find his spectacles. Ann, 13, felt it must be great fun being a grandparent because you can sleep in the afternoon!

From a group of nine-year-olds came the idea that grandparents are very old and tired and need a lot of rest. It was observed that they don't have to work so much and pensioners get into movies at half price. Peter asked, 'Why would they want to go to movies?' Others thought they went to bed too early and didn't know how to plug in the computer. They provided money for houses and got diseases like arthritis. From a more positive aspect, children felt grandparents went to football and shows together and often made crafts at home.

WHAT THE GRANDCHILDREN DON'T LIKE

As the children spoken to came from several different countries, they preferred their parents to speak English at home and got annoyed when they spoke their native tongue. In fact, some of the children were teaching their grandparents English.

They didn't like to be told constantly to wash their hands and to eat their pizzas with a knife and fork. They also said their grandparents were often cranky and told them to keep quiet. Ted mentioned that his grandmother would ask him a question and then answer it herself. Jake said he couldn't bear knitting or shopping and didn't like to just sit around doing nothing.

A great deal of curiosity was expressed over the false teeth seen in the glass when Amy stayed over. She was also amused at the funny underwear, red lips and gold fillings. Jane said her grandfather could watch television when he was asleep and her grandmother smelled of mothballs.

We tend to define who is old from the perspective of where we stand. A teenager is old to a child who is six. Mary, at 70, didn't want to go into a home where there were 80-year-olds. 'They're too old for me,' she said. Children know that grandparents are older than parents and like them to look that way. But perhaps not quite like the grandmothers in this poem from Colin Hawkin's *Granny Book*.

> *Often wicked tales are told*
> *Of grannies being very old.*
> *Hard of hearing, poor of sight*
> *With teeth that can no longer bite.*
> *Stiff old joints and snow-white hair*
> *But don't believe them*
> *They're not fair.*

Do some of the tales still stay with grandchildren when they ask why you are so wrinkly and will they have whiskers when they grow up? Or ask if their hair will go grey or drop off? We need to be honest with them — but we also need to show them how grandparents have changed through the years.

HINTS FOR GRANDPARENTS

- Lower expectations and give unconditional love.
- Open communication by listening and talking.
- Say no when appropriate.
- Only give advice when wanted.
- Offer practical help when possible.
- Remember you are not the parent.
- Have fun and enjoy your time together.
- Attend school functions and sports when invited.
- Be respectful, giving understanding and empathy.
- Try not to undermine adult children's parenting.
- Share some history of the 'old' days. Get out the photo album.
- Give comfort, love and experience.
- Don't play one grandchild against another. (Ava, now in her early forties, mentioned how her brother was always held up to her as an example of 'perfection' by her grandparents. 'Why can't you get on at school like Peter? How come you're so disorganised — Peter isn't.' She still carries the resentment.

TIME ALONE

The best way to get to know a grandchild is to spend time with them individually. In this way, they can get undivided attention, be the centre of attraction and feel very important. Being on their own avoids the distractions of others around. Only that person's needs will be attended to. It gives an opportunity to talk and enjoy each other's company and, in this way, the relationship can be enriched. Special outings can be arranged and, even though it takes time to work through a big family, one by one, it is worthwhile and can do wonders for self-esteem.

Without the special attention, children in large families particularly, often become quiet and withdrawn — or, on the other hand, yell and argue all the time. They try to get attention by showing off, by being pushy or loud, and doing silly things to irritate. With special time for themselves, grandchildren feel valued and will be more likely to respect and follow your modelling.

PARENTING THE PARENT

Are you able to receive from others, or are you used to being a giver? Try to accept help from others when it is offered and needed. A helping hand is comforting when you are sick or tired. This can also be an important time — a time for a reversal of roles, when adult children can parent their parents. Sometimes, wonderful offers are made by adult children. John was given a holiday cruise on a ship by his daughter, which he could not have afforded himself. Beth loves the theatre and has been given a subscription ticket for the year by her family. How wonderful it is to have outings and get-togethers organised by one's adult children.

As grandparents, you can now renew your relationship with your own children, for there is now a sense of equality in all being parents. However, as rapidly as the world is changing, so too is the family and it is well to keep in mind that there are certain things we can do nothing about. This can be a difficult feeling. The Serenity Creed used by Alcoholics Anonymous is helpful. 'God, grant me the serenity to accept the things I cannot change, the courage to change the things I can, and the wisdom to know the difference.'

This is my grandfather planting seeds and me accidently making a pair of shorts fall on him!

Paulo (8 yrs)

Teaching my grandpa to surf
Marcus (9 yrs)

CHAPTER 6

Losses are a part of life

> *Birth is the beginning*
> *Death the destination*
> *Life the journey.*
>
> **From a Jewish prayer book**

from the moment we are expelled from the safe, warm comfort of the womb into the bright lights and harsh noises of the world, to the time of our death, we incur losses. Playing peek-a-boo (now you see me, now you don't) can be emotionally upsetting for babies, and weaning can be seen as a loss for both mother and child. Have you noticed how little ones are uncertain and weepy when you leave the room? I saw a mother on the beach, trying to go into the water to have a swim. Her two-year-old was anxious and started to cry because of the separation. I still recall when I was aged three, and attending the party of my ten-year-old brother. There was a large communal cracker which burst into the sky, spewing presents into the air. My little legs weren't quick enough and I was left behind without a package. Amazing how that loss is still with me. What about the loss of a tooth around the age of five? The tooth fairy has to be summoned immediately to repair the damage! It is not as simple for other life events.

When I asked members of a group of grandparents to list the peaks and valleys of their lives on a life graph, these were some of the losses mentioned. (The gains are listed in Chapter 8, on Enrichment.)

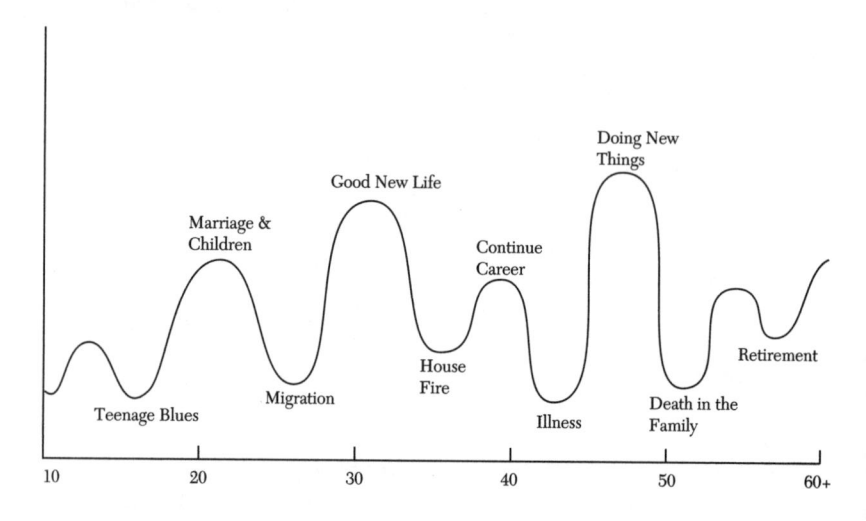

[Life graph showing peaks and valleys from age 10 to 60+: Teenage Blues, Marriage & Children, Migration, Good New Life, House Fire, Continue Career, Illness, Doing New Things, Death in the Family, Retirement]

LOSSES

- ousted by a new sibling
- migration, losing a homeland
- losing a house in a fire
- deteriorating health
- loss of self-esteem
- loss of freedom (concentration camps)
- retirement
- death of a friend or family member
- loss of memory, appearance
- death of a pet
- abortion
- unemployment
- first day at school
- empty nest
- loss of youth
- loss of money
- divorce

I will deal with some of the losses that are pertinent to grandparents now. (Divorce is mentioned in Chapter 7.)

MIGRATION

Migration is like an amputation, leaving raw nerve endings. Gone are the familiar sights, sounds and smells. I remember going to the Thirlmere train musuem in New South Wales, and sitting in a compartment of one of the old trains. The strong smell of red dust was a reminder of travelling through the desert in my old homeland in Africa. Where are the family and friends? Who am I and where am I? My identity is shattered. Those are the sorts of questions that migrants ask themselves. Often they have to learn a different language and find it hard to communicate with those around them. Some grandparents are still lost in some ancestral village and find their grandchildren disinterested in the past, having new values and being very Australianised. There is a barrier in communication and the young can outstrip the old in education and intellect.

Nick and Christina had come from a small island in Greece. Their marriage had been prearranged. They felt quite isolated in Australia. The lifestyle was different and they found their grandchildren's generation quite bewildering. Language and values bore no similarity to the past and they sometimes had a feeling that the grandchildren looked down on them. It was difficult for them to make contact. This is not an easy situation for any of the different generations and a great deal of tension occurs as traditions change and old values come into conflict. As a result, we also lose a lot of folklore and our family tradition and culture.

Diana Kidd has dealt very positively and skilfully with this problem in her book, *The Day Grandma Came to Stay*. An Italian grandmother comes to visit and Lucy is most resentful that she has to give up her room. She feels her parents wouldn't 'notice her even if she was covered with measles spots'. Nanna, an old lady, arrives dressed in black and Lucy cannot understand her and is annoyed that she is prevented from doing a lot of her own things because of her grandmother's visit. By the end of the book, there is a good relationship with Nanna and she has learnt something of her Italian heritage. She also acquires some knowledge of wines, fishnets and pasta.

Time is often needed to mourn the loss of a homeland and then the gains can be quite considerable. A new, free life, a different career, new and interesting people — and sometimes just being able to get out of a comfortable rut. Australia has seen a great deal of immigration since World War ll, and has been enriched in the process.

AGEING

'I'm less agile, I've done it all before and I am bored. I'm putting on weight, and where is the enjoyment?' Have you heard anyone say this — may be even yourself? With ageing, there is a sense of slowing down. Physical appearance can change and the hair turns grey. Aren't we known by some as the wrinklies? We lose brain cells, which do not get replaced, from the moment we are born. These are all losses in a sense — but there are gains in the later years. For a start, there is no longer any need to make an impression. You can be your authentic self and say what you like, enjoy reduced responsibility and far more freedom. Even loss of memory can be an advantage. And you don't have to listen to something you don't want to hear. (In Chapter 8, on Enrichment, we will be looking at further gains.)

RETIREMENT

We would first have to work on society itself to change the attitude to retirement. It seems that once you leave your employment you have little value. There is a feeling that you *used to be* a teacher, engineer, doctor, bus driver, lawyer, postman, and so on. What are you now? You are still the same person with the same qualifications. When asked who we are, we usually answer in terms of our work. This ties in with attitudes to children as they are growing up. Their worth is measured by what they achieve, not by what they are as humans.

Many people, particularly men, have everything invested in their jobs. Friends, interests and stimulation are often only to be found at work. When they retire, it is not easy to adjust to domestic life. One woman said she married her husband for better for worse, but not for lunch (of course, some lonely people would welcome someone for lunch). Her husband is constantly under her feet. He complains that there is dust behind the chair, the cheese she bought is cheaper at another supermarket and there are too many opened milk cartons in the fridge! The relationship at home can start to deteriorate.

Retirement affects people in different ways. Barbara, in her seventies, said it was the best time of her life. On the other hand, Fred was just dreading the day when he would have to leave his medical practice. Some people are retiring earlier these days, which can leave up to 25 years ahead. That is certainly a very long time to be sitting in an armchair doing very little.

Men often suffer from depression and loss of self-esteem, especially if they haven't prepared themselves through the years with new interests and hobbies. Their reduced activity gives them an empty feeling and they can feel worthless and useless. Their daily routine is different. The people, the places they visit, their clothes and food may all have changed. They may have a hard time finding a purpose in life and an identity — although some men say they have done their bit and just want peace and quiet. As Adele Horin writes, 'For this generation, whose lives have been defined by gender roles, men's retirement can starkly highlight a couple's different need for involvement.'

Some women are protected from the adverse effects of retirement. There is no retirement from homemaking and they often have a variety of interests. They are usually younger than their spouses (if they have one) and are into new ventures. They may be starting a new job and moving forwards while their partners are going down, sometimes from great heights. Women also have an ability to share feelings and thoughts with a friend over coffee. The older-generation man would only do this if he had a specific purpose, such as talking about business or sport.

Grandparents in their retirement can be invaluable to grandchildren. They can share a host of skills. John, an ex-English teacher, helped his grandson with homework, and Leesa started teaching German, her mother tongue, to Anna, aged five. William, a music teacher, was able to take pupils after school. Manual skills, such as sewing, carpentry, art and typing can taught and shared with grandchildren. Or, perhaps a game of chess to keep the brain active, or simply just for fun.

Retirement can be a big loss, but it is also an opportunity to do the new things you secretly wanted to do and didn't have a chance to do before. It can also liberate from career pressure and competition. (In Chapter 8, on Enrichment, lots of ideas are suggested.) For some, full-time political or neighbourhood activity on behalf of the community can be stimulating, and can be a continuation of what was engaged in previously. Early preparation for this new phase of life is important.

MONEY ISSUES

Nest eggs have a habit of dwindling in the later years and income is often considerably lessened. One of the greatest threats when growing older can be poverty. There is a need to organise and plan finances and to have a budget of assets and liabilities. Knowledge of whether you qualify for a pension is important. Your right to a pension depends on either an income test or an assets test. In Australia, the age pension is paid to men who are 65 or older, and to women who are 60 and over. The latter is in danger of being raised to 65.

Grandparents love to treat their grandchildren but can be worried sometimes about how they will survive. Banks and building societies produce kits and booklets offering financial guidance to people nearing the end of their working lives, or for those already in retirement.

WANING HEALTH

The word 'health' comes from the root word 'whole' which indicates a total style of living. The emotional, physical and mental sides of a person are all interlinked, despite the fact that we are getting more and more specialists who are treating only specific parts of the body, like the big toe of the left leg! Attitude is important in coping with any ills, but the best way to keep reasonably fit is prevention. It is possible to make illnesses that cause disability in the later years much less severe. To achieve this, certain aspects of lifestyle may have to be altered and appropriate activities engaged in.

Although sometimes we cannot prevent actual illness there is a lot we can do to maintain good health.

Physical problems — what can we do?
- Choose your doctor. It is important to ask questions.

He/she can advise you on health care.

• Optimal use of medication. Know what and how much you are taking, and why. It was reported in *The Age* of Melbourne, that 20 per cent of hospital admissions of older people are due to the fact that they have taken medication incorrectly.

• Exercise — walking and swimming, relaxation and yoga, stretching programs. This can improve fitness and lead to a feeling of well-being. Exercise can lower anxiety levels, reduce depression, improve the efficiency of the heart and lower blood pressure. It is also good for the creaking joints. Is that enough incentive to jump out of bed early in the morning and head for the parks? It is said that the left and right feet are life extenders.

• Check and monitor blood pressure.

• Attend to minor ills. Many of the things that worry us need only minor correction, for example, eyes, ears, teeth, skin nutrition, bladder and back.

• Eat a sensible diet — even if you think oats and bran taste like cattle food!

• Sleep. Don't toss and turn. Get a warm drink or put on some music. You often need less sleep than you think. Television can be disturbing in the middle of the night — it's too stimulating.

• Look for a good clean environment, smoke and pollution free. Not so easy to find!

Emotional health

• Express feelings, both positive and negative.

• Initiate friendship with smiles and greetings. When you see people walking in the street they can look very grim. Have you ever stood in a lift where everybody is staring at the ceiling? Who will break the ice?

- Be loving and accepting.
- Take risks and be trusting.

Mental health

- Begin tasks you have meant to do — and haven't, and feel good about it.
- Live in the NOW.
- Start new interests — have a positive attitude. This will reduce loneliness which can be so much a part of the later years.
- Use energy wisely and be selective. You can say 'No' as well as 'Yes'.
- Go at your own pace.
- Brain train — mental stimulation, challenges and projects.
- People and enjoyment are more important than things like housework. It will still be there tomorrow. Wendy always felt obliged to make the beds and clean the house before leaving home even if she missed out on something interesting. Exceptionally high standards of perfection in any area inevitably bring stress and disappointment.
- Have your own quiet time and indulge yourself — not too much chocolate cake, but maybe a foam bath, a good book or a cold beer.
- Strike a balance between looking after yourself and others.
- Devise a drill for your memory. Eena Job in her book, *Fending off Forgetfulness*, suggests a routine check to see you have everything for the day's activities. Purse, tick, umbrella, tick, books, tick, glasses, tick, keys, tick, and so on. A bit like a pilot checking the controls before take-off.

These preventive measures may help a little to reduce

some of the health risks of the later years.

There are certain diseases that medical science is still working on. Because our life expectancy has risen so much, Alzheimers disease has reared its ugly head. For families, this is a very sad and difficult disease to handle. Grandchildren need to be given honest and open answers to their questions. A simple explanation that Gran has Alzheimers and it is not catching is enough. Explain that it is caused by changes in the brain and is a disease, that she will be confused, won't necessarily remember the family and may feel frightened. Knowing the facts, children are able to cope better even though it is very hard to watch someone you love change so. Holding a hand is still possible even though there may not be any reaction. Leah said that her grandchildren accepted her husband's deterioration better than she did and they were extremely helpful and buoyant.

The good news is, that an American scientist has discovered a gene associated with the risk of developing Alzheimers disease — which may give some clue to prevention. Losing your memory occurs progessively through life and is not necessarily a precursor of Alzheimers.

In the US, only 5 per cent of people over the age of 65 and 20 per cent over 80 have Alzheimers, (the figures are roughly the same in Australia) indicating that it is a disease not just normal ageing. This is illustrated by the following: Joss asked Mary, at the celebration of her 75th birthday, if she was interested in the hereafter. 'Yes' she said. 'I go into the lounge room and ask myself — what am I hereafter?' This happens to many of us.

DEATH OF A PARTNER

This is the ultimate loss. For some partners who have been

together for 30, 40, or perhaps 50 years it is hard even to contemplate a life alone. Gone is the companionship, sharing, sexuality and intimacy. In the United Kingdom, one in two women are widows by the age of 65 and one in six men are widowers. Men particularly feel they are not entitled to grieve. They have to be strong, wear a mask and take care of everybody else. In all this there can be an overwhelming feeling of loneliness.

Loneliness

Loneliness is a scourge in the western world. People may have little close contact with others —particularly those in big cities who live in high-rise, anonymous-looking buildings. Dave, a widower, said he welcomed seeing the postman each day (not that he received any letters) as that was the only time he could have a conversation. This contact made him realise that there was still a world out there.

People deal with loneliness in different ways. Some cope by withdrawing, not wanting to show others how much their loss hurts. They go inside themselves and become depressed. They also hope someone might come and rescue them. Others become busy-holics, having an activity for each minute of the day or night. If they are still working, they work long hours and go out with people they don't necessarily like just for the distraction. Running in every direction and gobbling up everyone in sight is a way of getting through the lonely hours.

Mourning

In our society, we are not taught to identify and express our feelings. If you cry, friends want to cheer you up, if you don't seem too upset you may be described as strong and brave. It is healthy and appropriate to express feelings. If we are not permitted and encouraged to do so, we can carry large and heavy invisible bags full of loss on our backs, which will finally weigh us down.

Granny Shirley described how she felt when her husband died. 'I was like a big whale being beached and gasping for air. I was floundering until such time as I could get back into the water.'

Ruth Park, in *Fishing in the Styx* , says, 'to be wonderful is to handle grief badly'. She was admired for her calmness and courage when her husband died but found herself suffering within. As she writes, 'so mourning is not done, and the tears that run down inside turn to acid that may corrode your soul for years.'

STAGES IN LOSS

T I M E

SHOCK / DENIAL → ANGER / GUILT → DEPRESSION → GRIEF / SADNESS → RE-ORGANISE / RECOVERY

H O P E

Elizabeth Kubler Ross suggests that most people go through stages in their grieving.

- Denial — It can't be happening to me. It happens to other people.
- Anger, Guilt — It is not fair. Maybe I should have done

something different.
- Bargaining — If I do such and such, it will go away.
- Depression, sadness, loneliness — It is getting worse. I'll never get through it.
- Acceptance — Reorganising and trying to move on

These stages can be interchangeable and differ from one individual to another. They often appear in all sorts of losses. The passage of time can help in the healing process.

Having gone through the grief experience of shock, (especially if the loss was sudden), anger and enormous sadness, grandparents can start to face reality, as painful as it is. The real healing process starts with the funeral and continues as long as it is necessary. Families rally round and grandchildren can help to lighten the leaden atmosphere, as well as be there to cry together.

This little poem by Anna Cummins says a lot.

> *Do not save your loving speeches*
> *For your friends till they are dead*
> *Do not write them on their tombstones*
> *Speak them rather now instead.*

Memories

As Proust said, 'Mourning is a transition from grief to memory.'

Death is very final but nobody can take away memories. Often grandchildren are reminders of the departed. John, age eight, is musical like his grandmother. Jane, age 12, has thick hair like her grandfather had. In a sense, grandparents are immortal because genes are passed on from one generation to another.

Memories keep the grandparents alive. Photographs, diaries, letters and oral history are invaluable. Before he died, Harold made tapes of his life in Europe and Australia so that he could be remembered. His wife asked friends to write anecdotes of their personal memories for a communal album. Memories of friends and family are often carried around in our heads and remain for some time to come. They are very precious.

DEATH OF A GRANDCHILD

When a child dies, it is devastating for the whole family. We often ask, Why? And we get no answers. For grandparents, it is hard to understand why the young die before them. It does not fit the natural order of things and they may feel a sense of guilt for surviving.

The death is tragic, whether the child was a baby, toddler, at school, an adolescent or a young adult, or whether death was from a long protracted illness or sudden. The pain is always great. An enormous amount of love and care is needed to go through the grieving days. Being surrounded by close family and friends can bring a sense of comfort and strength. Wendy, whose baby had died at six weeks, just liked to sit holding hands with people she loved — not necessarily talking, but feeling a great physical warmth and rapport.

Grandparents in a grieving family can help enormously. There are practical things they can help with, like keeping the household going, shopping, cooking, answering the phone and looking after the other children. Emotionally, they can help just by being there to listen or to cry together. Remembering the skills suggested in Chapter 3, Open your Ears and Close your Mouth, can be helpful.

In a sense, losing a grandchild is a double loss for grandparents. On the one hand, seeing their adult child in pain, hurt and desolate, and on the other, feeling bereft and experiencing their own personal loss of a loved grandchild. Jim, who had made a strong relationship with his grandson, aged 11, found it extremely hard to accept that he would no longer be there for their football games in the backyard, or fishing expeditions on the high seas. He looked after the rest of the family, but later became quite depressed.

Parents and grandparents and, in fact, whole families need to grieve and move at their own pace. Well-wishers often try to cheer up friends which is often more to do with their own discomfort with unhappiness. People grieve in different ways. Some express feelings openly, others cover up and do it in their own way. The grieving process could take months or years — or never get resolved. Mal McKissock, in his book *Coping with Grief*, outlines the possible reactions and responses to loss and how to get through the grieving times.

Grandparents often put their needs aside to console their adult children. However, there comes a time when they also need the opportunity to cry, be angry and feel sad. Looking around at the world and other people's grandchildren can trigger many feelings. Jean, whose grandchild had died from Sudden Infant Death Syndrome, said everytime she saw a small baby in a pram it brought back memories of what had happened to her grandchild.

A family tree planting ceremony can be very healing. At the time of Neil's death, at the age of 13, his family planted a white magnolia tree. Now, every August, the white blooms burst forth, giving a sense of renewal and hope.

DEATH OF A GRANDPARENT

Although this is more in the order of things, the death of a grandparent can be the first major loss a child experiences.

It can be quite traumatic.

Children need to be told what has happened and be permitted to attend the funeral, if possible. In days gone by, children were sent away during that time and came back wondering where their beloved grandparents were. Dan, age four, went to the funeral of his grandfather. On the way back from the cemetery, the family stopped for a pizza. Dan wanted to know if Gramps would come soon to eat his pizza. His concept of death was impermanence but it was healthy for him to say what he thought and be part of the family mourning.

Death is a time to draw the family together for support and affection. Their questions need to be answered simply and honestly. Bill, age five, talked about his grandfather's death and wanted to know if he would still be coming to his birthday party. We can often take a lesson from children in their ability to be so open and honest. It was explained to Bill that his grandfather was dead and wouldn't be coming back, and that they were left on earth to carry on and remember his love. Bill turned around and said 'Can I go now and play with Ned?' Ned was the family's dog. Children know just how much they can take.

Grandparents and parents can help children to become familiar with the cycle of nature. In this way, they can gain a knowledge of birth and death. John, age 10, had a budgie with a big tumour on his throat. The budgie died on the operating table and John was devastated. The budgie was wrapped in a cloth and buried in the garden under a large oak tree. A short funeral service was held and John cried buckets, but soon ran off to kick his football.

Childrens' concept of death

Children's concept of death varies depending on their age.

Babies can show signs of sorrow, sadness and depression. When a carer is no longer there they experience a sense of loss. They can withdraw from the world by not responding, they may grow quieter and be very tearful.

Children aged one to four usually know something is wrong. Everyone is unhappy. They see a dead insect or bird which stops moving and realise it is not alive. They regard death as not permanent and may believe the person will come back. They are somewhat mystified and need simple and honest answers.

With the ages of five to eight, there is more of a realisation of the finality of death and they sometimes console the parents. There are often lots of questions and they need to be given information when wanted. Paul, age six, wanted to know if grandpa would get wet and cold lying in the cemetery.

Between the ages of eight to twelve, there is a fear of separation and the possibility that it could happen to someone close in the family — or even to themselves. At this stage, they need a reassurance that they are not going to die, as death usually happens when people are older or sick. After his younger brother died, Jeremy, age 12, had difficulty going to sleep at night in case he stopped breathing.

Teenagers are very wrapped in their egos and do not necessarily express their feelings or indicate what is going on inside. This does not mean they feel any less. In fact, they may be over-anxious and sometimes react in an extreme way. Bryan Mellanie and Robert Ingpen's book Lifetimes starts off with the following:

> *There is a beginning*
> *and an ending for everything*
> *that is alive.*
> *In between is living.*

They continue, in their wonderful book, to compare nature with the human cycle. And as we watch the seasons, the dead leaves in winter and the sprouting of green shoots in the spring, we become aware of loss, new life and regeneration.

Grandpa (Mum's Dad)
Kimberley (9 yrs)

CHAPTER 7
Variations on a Family Theme

*i*n our society, the extended family, where the old and the young live together in familiar neighbourhoods, no longer exists. There are so many changes and diversity of lifestyles in the modern family. Grandparents sometimes feel buffeted about and unsure of their roles and position.

FARAWAY GRANDPARENTS

The world is on the move and families are often parted. Grandparents are at the mercy of their adult children's mobility which can take them to exotic lands or to the four corners of the earth. Molly goes to Thailand to visit her family quite frequently and enjoys the change and stimulation. On the other hand, grandparents can spend a great deal of their time and energy globe-trotting in order to maintain a relationship with their grandchildren. When you have tasted the joys of being together, it is very hard to be separated and an emotional hole can develop. Not being able to watch the development of grandchildren and share the important milestones along the way is hard to bear. When I looked at the photos of my 15-month-old granddaughter, who I hadn't seen for almost a year, I felt a pang, not knowing her and wondering just how she really looked. Was her hair still that colour? How much did she have? Was she ready to walk? What, if anything, was she saying?

All or Nothing

Visiting, or being visited, by grandchildren has an all-or-nothing quality about it. For weeks before the visit, there are enormous preparations. Beds are made, special foods are bought and wonderful outings and treats planned. When they come, it is like an invasion and the home is turned upside-down. All personal needs and activities have to be put aside. There is no time for that quiet cup of tea, or the time for your favourite television or radio program. Different generations are generally unused to living together and not always accepting of each other's habits. The telephone rings incessantly — and not for us, and we see each other in an undiluted way. Then, when the time is up just as relationships have started to develop, and the demolition squad departs, there is an eerie silence. The hellos and goodbyes can be quite traumatic. There can be also a feeling of giving everything to compensate for the times they are not there. There is usually too much time together which is undiluted and then, when they have gone, no time together, which is unnatural. It can be very hard for grandparents to adjust to these changes.

Then there is the situation where grandparents do the visiting. Before they leave, they look for presents and feel a bit bewildered, not knowing what stages the children have reached and what their likes and dislikes are. It is a bit like beginning a novel in the middle and feeling a little lost. On arrival, there is all the excitement of being together but also the knowledge there has to be another parting. But, you can see where they work and play and keep a picture of them in your mind. It is often more practical being in a holiday place together where nobody is stressed or has big responsibilities. The worst thing for grandparents is just sitting around, dropping their normal activities and not knowing how to fit in with very different routines. When leaving, you can often come home with a great longing for those cuddles and happy times. It is much harder to maintain a natural relationship with grandchildren from a distance but there are certain ways of keeping in touch.

How to keep in touch

The telephone is a great help in hearing about personal triumphs, joys and disasters. I recall, when travelling overseas, receiving the big news that my grandson, age 5, had just lost a baby tooth. Videos bring you up to date with the development, appearance and sounds of the family. Letters, cards and special parcels are exciting. Dot wrote a long autobiography of her life in letters to her grandchildren. She said she felt she was there with them by proxy. Cuttings and titbits from magazines help to fill in the personal life picture. Audio tapes of children playing various instruments, singing, or just talking, bring them closer. Drawings are fun — as are surprise presents wrapped in bright-coloured papers. One grandparent received a lock of a grandchild's hair to show her the colour. The last time she had seen her grandchild she had had no hair! Paul exchanged lots of photos and cards and cuttings to do with cricket with his grandson.

Grandchildren reach an age when they are old enough to visit on their own. It is a wonderful way of enriching the relationship and doing joyful things together. Mary's 10-year-old grandchild came from another state. They went to films, galleries, craft places and enjoyed each other's company. Was it a coincidence that Mary went on a two-week holiday soon after? Was it to recuperate?

On the other hand, Molly's grandchildren, having been away for five years, decided to return home. In the meantime, Molly had learnt to live without them. Being on her own, she was used to the peace and quiet of living alone. Now, there is turmoil and noise and she is finding it hard to re-adjust to small children. As she says, 'It was difficult when the family was away and now they are home it is impossible'. A great deal of negotiation and working out will have to be done.

Mention must be made of grandparents who choose to move away themselves. They feel they deserve to enjoy their later years in their own way. This is especially prevalent in the US, where many retirement homes have been set up. (This is dealt with in Chapter 1.)

Rosa and Philip (both grandparents) decided to sail around the world in a yacht. They felt the family was managing just fine and that they were not needed. They visited each summer and kept up the contact with faxes and phone calls. Rosa elected to go to the warmer climate of northern Queensland, despite her family protestations. She wanted a chance to set up a life for herself and found it comfortable and peaceful, although she missed the grandchildren.

In all the ways mentioned, relationships between grandparents and grandchildren can be kept alive. Luckily the world is getting smaller. Trips can be made more easily and it is possible to keep in closer contact from afar.

DIVORCE

Today, 37 per cent of first marriages end in divorce and 55 per cent of second marriages. It is said that six per cent of second marriages end in separation within four years. In Australia, approximately 800 000 children are affected by divorce and remarriage, according to the Australian Institute of Family Studies.

There are no figures to show how this involves grandparents who find it hard to know how to behave and where they stand in the family. Often they are not aware of the break-up — or are not told until it happens. Adult children sometimes want to protect their parents and not disappoint them, or they want to cling on to their independence and so keep quiet. The one partner may decide to move to another state after the separation, or they may be embittered and want to cut off relationships with the other side of the family. Often the mother/daughter relationship is maintained but, when it is the son, the relationship can be diminished. On the whole, maternal grandparents are said to have much more contact with their grandchildren than paternal grandparents. Helen mentioned that her son was divorced and lived up north. She experienced a sense of loss and grief because she hardly ever saw the grandchildren and felt she was losing touch. It takes a lot of energy, courage and patience for grandparents to work out exactly what they can do. There can be ex-husbands and ex-wives but hopefully, not ex-parents or ex-grandparents.

Dilemmas of divorce

Not knowing which way to turn is one dilemma. Many grandparents have built up good relationships with the in-laws and don't want to lose them. They also don't want to jeopardise their relationships with their own adult children. Mavis was extremely fond of her daughter-in-law, and vice-versa. When the divorce came through, her son resented this relationship and didn't want his mother to go to the house and see the children. This caused a great deal of heartache. Other dilemmas are:

- Being afraid of losing contact with the grandchildren. This can happen, especially in a non-custodial situation where the in-laws have the children.
- How to cope with extreme emotional reactions when the family is in disarray. Self-esteem is at an all-time low. It is important not to take the anger in a personal way.
- Just watching it all happen and not being able to actively change anything.
- Losing legal access to the children.

What can you do?

- Be diplomatic. Stay out of parents' conflicts.
- Any practical help you offer is a bonus. Betty did a great deal of the driving to school and back. In this way, she also kept up the contact with the grandchildren. Financial help and babysitting is usually well received, as is attending school concerts, sports days, and other activities.
- Divorce can have a very acrimonious side and the grandchildren can be angry and bewildered. It is best to accept this and realise that it is not personal — and hopefully will pass.
- Make sure that the grandchildren are not used as a football in the middle. It is not a good idea to question them about the break-up, or take sides or ask them to be messengers. There is no need for any 'baddies' in all this, so criticism is unproductive.

- Allow grandchildren to be angry or sad, and express other negative feelings.
- In divorce, there is a great need for caring, reliable people who remain constant. Grandchildren can sleep over and find a haven with you at this particular time. Jack was doing the Higher School Certificate exam. He voluntarily moved to his grandparents while he was studying for the exams as there he found support and tranquillity.
- Take away blame, especially from the in-laws. There can be a feeling of hostility towards the adult child's partner.
- Realise that the initial stages of going through divorce can be very difficult. Later, the family begins to settle. It is a bit like having an operation and giving yourself time for recovery. Allow a period for everyone to readjust.

In one of the grandparenting groups, Minna mentioned her ex-daughter-in-law was getting remarried. She felt rather strange receiving an invitation, but decided to go. She had worked hard at the relationship so her acceptance was tinged with both sadness and joy. She attended the wedding and found that her strong positive feelings towards the bride over-rode her uncertainties as a result of the divorce. This made it much easier for her grandchildren, aged six and nine, who were there.

Loss of grandchildren in divorce

In Australia, there doesn't seem to be any legal provision for grandparents. If one of the parents decides the grandchildren are not to see their grandparents, they can apply to the Family Court, but so far it hasn't proved to be very helpful. This can be a very sad situation and the possibility of support groups is being discussed. Leila Friedman, in her book called *Why Can't I Sleep at Nana's Anymore?* has addressed this problem. In general, maternal grandparents benefit most in divorce situations. Grandparents' relationships with in-laws can drop off entirely.

In the US, the situation is a little different as there are special laws saying that grandparents can go to court to get visitation rights if the custodial parent refuses access. Some time ago, in Western Australia, a teenage boy divorced his parents. Perhaps, in the future, children will have the chance to have their say in not losing their grandparents.

In the television program, *Mother and Son*, someone says 'they don't need to see the grandchildren — after all they've got the photos.' The situation can be quite cruel.

There is a need to make sure grandchildren suffer as little as possible from the grandparents' side. It does mean that grandparents have to put their needs and feelings aside just at that particular moment. Not an easy matter. Supporting and keeping the communication lines open is all important. Keep sending the cards and letters — even if you get no feedback. There is still a chance that later that you will be remembered.

When one couple divorced, the daughter-in-law wouldn't let the grandparents see the grandchildren for several years. At the age of 15, the grandson made contact with them of his own free will and now visits them regularly.

When grandparents divorce

Adult children can be very disapproving when their parents divorce. They sometimes like things the way they used to be and aren't sure where they stand. They often wonder if they are losing their babysitters and how it will work for them. A great many of the suggestions mentioned for grandparents could be valid also for adult children.

Jean, 16, was extremely surprised, and even angry,

when she found her divorced grandmother was remarrying. She didn't think 'this sort of thing' happened to older people. She also worried that Granny could now be too busy to take her out on treats.

Divorce is a time of upheaval in families. However, it can also bring opportunites for closer ties with grandchildren and a better understanding of family members. Support and love is especially needed for grandchildren who are feeling abandoned and confused.

SINGLE PARENTS

So many parents today are struggling on their own as a result of divorce, or being widowed, or simply because they choose to. Thirteen per cent of families in Australia are single-parent families. They are working in all directions, twice as hard, in order to survive. Again, grandparents can play an enormous part in supporting the needs of the family both practically and emotionally. There are so many jobs to be done — babysitting, chauffering, cooking, shopping. The list is endless. Single parents can often have a very close bond with their children as they are together more, but these children can become adult far quicker than most, from sheer necessity. Single parents may welcome help, but they can also feel a bit possessive and use the children for company, shying away from others. Grandparents need to consider what life is like as a single parent, having to do everything on their own in a couple-orientated world. Joy said that on Fridays people used to say to her 'Have a good weekend', but nobody called. Life can be very lonely.

Grandma or Grandpa can act as a role model for the missing partner. They can also be a represention of the sex of the person who is not there. James lost his father when he was seven. His grandfather played an active male role in taking him to cricket and football. He also went with him on a father/son weekend.

STEPFAMILIES

As there is a high rate of divorce, second marriages have become prevalent. The result, in many cases, is stepchildren. Joy Conolly describes this phenomenon in her book *Step Families*, as when 'Family trees become Family forests'. Grandparents often become unsettled and disorientated. The number of grandchildren increases. What about all those different names? Apart from having difficulty in accepting a new marriage partner for their adult

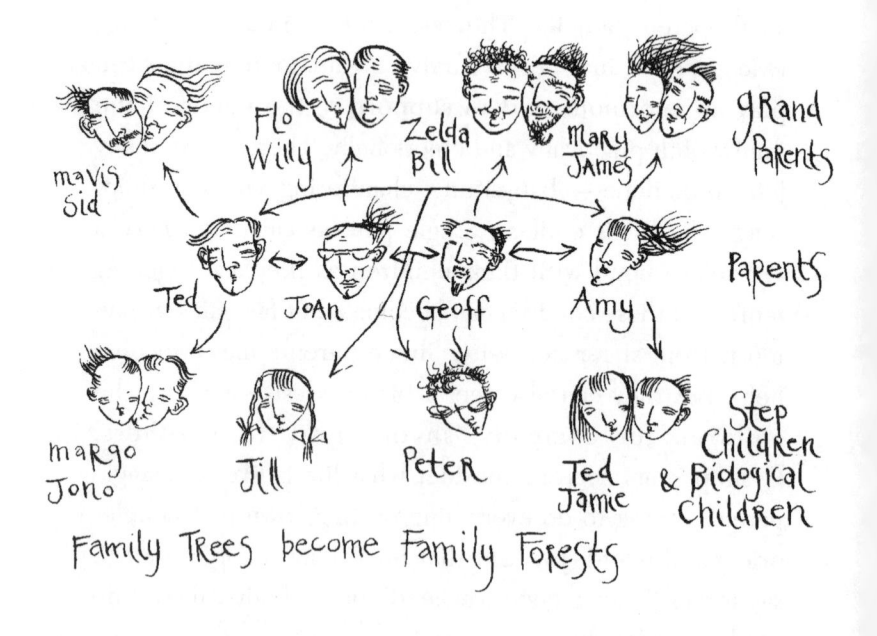

Family Trees become Family Forests

child, it is hard to know where to begin with the grandchildren. The idea of calling a stepfamily 'blended' is certainly a misnomer. There are all sorts of dynamics and variations.

Feelings of loyalty, rejection and resentment abound as stepfamilies are born from loss and require lots of understanding and friendship.

Kate, with two children, married Bill with three older children. These children had eight grandparents as the other spouses had also remarried. The mind boggles. At speech days and concerts, many rows were filled with this family and they managed to keep things on an amicable basis. This is not always possible and certainly *The Brady Bunch* gives a false idea of reality. The grandchildren can carry a great deal of anger from the divorces and deposit it on anyone around, including grandparents. Birthdays, anniversaries and special occasions are renowned for difficulties and certainly eat a hole in the pocket with six presents becoming twelve. Parents can be in competition with each other — as can the grandparents. At whose house is the family party? Who brings the food? Who picks up the children? What about presents? Who will be there? There is quite a lot to untangle.

The following questions were asked by some of the grandparents:
- I'm a stepgrandparent. How do I behave?
- What will they call me? Do I blunder in, or keep my distance?
- How do I form a relationship with children I have never met?
- How can I be fair with stepchildren and biological grandchildren?

It would be presumptous for anyone to think they know the answers, but here are a few suggestions.

- Let stepchildren know you are interested, but don't push in or interfere.

- Ask them what they would like to call you. See if it fits in with your idea.
- Take time getting to know each other. Old antagonisms are sometimes carried along. Don't take any hostility personally. Children are having to get through their own difficulties. For example, they may have been the eldest before and now they are in the middle, or even the youngest in the family. The symmetry has changed.
- Give practical support where possible. One grandfather, who is a retired doctor, gave science lessons to his stepgranddaughter and their relationship developed.
- Give support to the couple without hostility being projected onto the in-laws.
- Arrange outings for the children. What do they like? Do they like films, picnics, boating, museums or other activities. In this way you can get to know them.
- Don't discuss the previous divorces, or personal issues regarding the parents.
- Try to include new stepchildren without ignoring your own grandchildren, who may be jealous.

It is rather like a juggling act. The same sorts of difficulties can also arise with grandparents and adopted grandchildren – particularly if they were adopted at an older age. It is best to remember that everyone in the family is feeling their way and getting used to a new situation. It is also a possibility that you won't like one of the family members, or they won't like you — especially after being fed for years on the fairytale of Cinderella and her cruel stepmother. That's fine. You didn't choose them and they didn't choose you. Just aim for a working arrangement. It is a slow, gentle process and the main thing is to have respect for others and to be able to talk about the difficulties. There are as many solutions and variations as there are families.

SURROGATE GRANDPARENTS

Some children are deprived of loving for various reasons. The parents may be over-extended and have little time — or families may be in conflict. It is different in Aboriginal families where aunts and uncles take part in block parenting. The responsibility for the children does not rest just with the parents.

On the other hand, people in their later years may have lots of time and lots of love to give. The two generations can often be matched to bridge the gap and cross the age boundaries. At the same time, countless older people have no relations and welcome the idea of joining another family.

In divorce, when grandparents have difficulties with access to grandchildren, they may enjoy giving to other children — and at the same time receive a great deal themselves.

Betty, a young mother of two girls, was divorced. She lived in a block of units where two older people befriended her. They babysat, took the children on outings, and became very close to the family. Betty was estranged from her own parents and found this relationship very comforting. People who are migrants and have no extended family can also benefit from similar arrangements. At school gatherings, surrogate grandparents often fill in the gap when there are no grandparents.

In Michigan, in the US, home-bound senior citizens are matched with 'latch-key' children who normally return to empty homes at the end of a day. The children call the surrogate grandparents on the phone about homework or other matters. In this way, the children feel more wanted and don't have to disturb parents at work. The system is called 'Latchmatch'.

In this way, elders can get a feeling of being needed again. John, a surrogate grandfather, went to all the football games with Ted, age nine. He taught him carpentry while his wife enjoyed going to films and concerts with them. Shirley, who had no grandchildren herself, was very involved with her sister's grandchildren and they had a real love for her. She would also gladly listen to all the talk of their wonderful exploits and achievements and didn't mind her sister being a granny bore. Surrogate grandparents have a great deal to offer.

Job Advertisement
- Are you a person with some time to give to others?
- Have you some spare love ?
- Can you lend an ear?

If you answer yes to these three questions, you would make a very good surrogate grandparent.

The Volunteer Centre has provided a scheme for seniors to go into the schools to help children with reading, relate their experiences of the past and generally give some special attention to the pupils. Rewarding and close relationships can be built in this way. Children blossom with individual attention.

On their part, schools arrange for the young to visit the hospitals and retirement homes so there is an interchange of generations. The children sing, take flowers, tell stories and make very warm relationships.

An organisation called 'Aunties and Uncles' exists which provides a family network for people who have no family support. It is organised on a voluntary basis with government support. Surrogate relatives take out children one weekend a month and are able to give some extra love and attention. Older people are sometimes part of the scheme and benefit from the relationships formed.

Work is still being done on schemes to liase children with surrogate grandparents. There are some difficulties in supervision on both sides and more headway has been achieved in England and the US. Building a relationship between the young and the old can have enormous benefits. The children see that growing old can be a positive experience and not necessarily the dreary picture that society often presents. They also receive more cuddles, love and attention. On the grandparents side, there is companionship, a feeling of being needed and having lots of fun. Let's hope that soon there will be a Dial-a-Grandparent like there is Dial-a-Mum. In Queensland, an Adopt-a-Granny unit has been set up. People are matched by the amount of time they can give, their religion, age and personalities. Grandfathers are also applying.

IN-LAWS

It has to be realised that we have a long history with our biological children. We only meet our daughters and sons-in-law somewhat later and they have to get used to us. More work has to be put in to get to know them and sometimes there is no great love on either side. However, some effort can be made to accept differences in a family and to make things workable.

Parents usually control the level of contact with grandchildren and their grandparents. If relationships were good before between father/son and mother/daughter they are more likely to continue that way. This can affect daughters and sons-in-law. Very often, the husbands tend to go along with their wives if there are bad vibes, else they are caught in the middle. However, we have to realise the grandchiildren aren't just our childrens' but somebody else's too.

With grandparents themselves, there can be a great deal of competition to woo the grandchildren. Jilly Cooper calls it Granny-mosity. Who can give the best present? Who brings the yummiest chocolates? Who smooches up to the grandchildren? Who can give the most time or outings? One grandmother took out her brag book of photographs in the middle of a dinner party and proceeded to bore the company with details of each grandchild. She seemed to think she had a tribe of geniuses. The yawns at the table appeared to go undetected. She also stressed the invaluable part she played — not like the other grandmother who was working and wasn't as available.

In-laws need time to get to know each other. They may be from different cultures, speak different languages or have different values. They too may not like each other. After all, they did not choose to be together. Again, some working arrangement can be helpful for the family, otherwise they get tugged in all directions. Jim mentioned that he wouldn't visit his daughter if her in-laws were there. This was an extra burden for her and needed to be sorted out. They found a solution in having different visiting times and agreed to come together only on very important occasions. They all agreed they could be civil to each other for short periods. Young parents can often find themselves in the middle of a feud and patience and effort is often needed on both sides.

Families change in so many ways and there are certainly many variations on a theme. To make 'sweet music', it is necessary to have some flexibility and to try new ideas for size to avoid too many discords. It is always possible for families to come together in times of difficulties, although the path may appear to be quite hazardous. Sustaining that closeness is not easy.

In his small poem, Sir Thomas Brown depicts the strength of human beings.

> *Life is a pure flame*
> *And we live*
> *As if by an invisible sun*
> *Burning within us.*

My grandparents
Abbie (12 yrs)

CHAPTER 8
From Stress to Enrichment

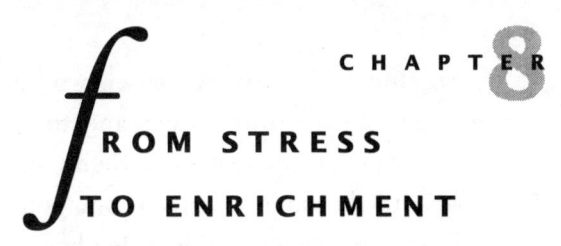

> *Time and Personal energy*
> *Is the coin of your life*
> *It is the only coin you have*
> *Be careful lest someone else*
> *spends it for you.*
>
> **Carl Sandberg**

*O*ur society emphasises productivity and life is considered meaningless without it. Young children are reprimanded when they daydream. Their worth is often measured by what they do and what they achieve rather than the sort of people they are. This yardstick also applies to people in the later years, especially when parental responsibilities are over and after retirement. Yet this is the perfect opportunity to feel valued as a person and not just as a producer. Does meeting a friend for coffee to enhance friendship, or doing a course for sheer interest, not have value?

Han Suyin wrote, 'Enjoy the season, lift your head. Take your delight in momentariness, flowers and friends unnoticed.'

This is very pertinent to elders, who have more free

time to stop and stare. However, we have never been taught take pleasure in things and to enjoy ourselves. Margaret said that when she was young, she felt she had to apologise to the table when she bumped it. Thinking of herself was outrageous, and enjoying herself was out of the question. Today's grandparents are perhaps the first generation to deal with the reality of free time and retirement. As life expectancy has increased there are many more years to productively fill. The old work ethic makes adults believe that their free time has to be organised activities and duties, rather than enjoyment. The recreation business is booming but it needs to be realised that it is important to play and participate for the pure pleasure of it. This can be very difficult for grandparents who have worked all their lives, or looked after other people. It is important to consider and value ourselves. The old message of 'don't be selfish' is hard to eradicate, especially if it has been drummed constantly into our heads. Grandma Jane, from one of our groups, said that only now does she realise that she deserves time off and that she has a right to enjoy herself. For years, she carried a feeling of guilt from her mother who only wanted her to care for others. It was unthinkable that she did anything for herself.

Grandparents need to look after themselves and not look only to the family for supplying their stimulation and interests. Time must be satisfying, not depleting. Handling stress, which is an inevitable part of life, is important. Learning to deal with the pressures of everyday living is vital before you are able to get out, enjoy and enrich.

STRESS

Stress means pressure and tension in response to certain life events. It is the wear and tear of everyday life. It comes from inside and outside and we often feel powerless in coping. Look around at people in the street. Faces are lined with tension and bodies are bent and distorted. Children sit stiffly at classroom desks and are physically and mentally confined to long hours of study. We often deal with stress in the way we have been programmed through the years by getting sick, being frenetic, feeling depressed or choosing an alternative lifestyle.

Having no stress at all brings boredom and this can become yet another stress factor. This is prevalent in the later years when people feel there is no more meaning to life. Families may have gone and there is little stimulation left. They are retired and feel no self-value. For some retirees, their whole sense of security and value was based around work. Loss of this closes an outlet for self-expression. The nursing homes and retirement villages are sometimes like waiting rooms for the dying and people talk about 'killing time'. Unless we reach out and take the initiative, life can be worthless. Stress depends on a number of things to do with personality, previous experiences and value put on activities. The idea is not to avoid stress, but to make sure we live with it in a positive way that gives pleasure, fulfilment and satisfaction.

Some stress signals

Physical
- Increased heart rate
- Dermatitis
- Dizziness and headaches
- Tiredness
- Tight chest, neck or back muscles
- Being accident prone
- Vomiting

- Elevated blood pressure
- Trembling or twitching
- Frequent minor illnesses

Emotional
- Irritable and depressed
- Restless, lack of interest
- Crying frequently
- Angry with the world
- Bad dreams
- Withdrawal and low self-value

Mental
- Being forgetful and preoccupied
- Less active and creative
- Less able to concentrate
- Living in the past

In times of stress, people often eat and drink more. If they are smokers they smoke more and sweet eaters raid the lolly tins. Others starve themselves and can't be bothered to eat. Some constantly pop pills or sleep too much. What can we do?

Physical

Exercise, good nutrition and adequate sleep is essential. Waking up in the middle of the night (when I have my biggest worries and my most brilliant ideas) can be helped by relaxation and meditation. If this isn't done the next day can often be a write-off. It is also important to attend to minor ills and not neglect teeth, hearing, eyes, skin and blood pressure. Spend as much time in clean air as possible. Listen to your body and rest when tired or unwell. Keep away from drugs as much as possible.

Laughter lowers anxiety levels and tests have shown that it speeds up the heart rate. It also relieves muscle tension particularly in the face, diaphragm and abdomen, and can be a positive release of feelings.

Emotional

Expressing feelings is important as they can get stuck inside and come out as headaches, ulcers and numerous aches and pains. Being assertive and learning to say 'no' can prevent resentment and the horrible pain in the pit of the stomach, the stiff neck or the heavy chest. Love and friendship help a great deal — this may have to be sought out, which also means trusting others. Some people find it hard to receive. All their lives they have been on the giving end. There is a feeling of unworthiness connected to this. Grandparents need to recognise their value and realise that most people also like to give to them and there needs to be some balance between giving and receiving. How I enjoy my adult children inviting me for dinner, or the grandchildren unravelling my computer problems.

Mental

I often find that I am either quite frenetic or not occupied at all. There needs to be a balance between being overcommitted and undercommitted. Energy must be selective. Grandparents often feel very stressed when they have said 'yes' indiscriminately and are rushing around in all directions in order to please everybody.

Talking to yourself can be helpful — ask yourself, must this be done so often? Can it be done differently? Is it really necessary? Can it be done by someone else?

I find, as the years pass, that I have less tolerance for things I don't enjoy. Going to a bad theatre play or to a disastrous party can be a waste of time and energy. Quantitively, energy is reduced in the later years so it is important to use it for life's satisfaction.

Stretching to embrace new activities and interests, and adopting a positive attitude to life is a help. I do not want to play down the difficulties of coping with illness but some mental relaxation, some self-indulgence and tender loving care from others will do wonders.

We all vary as to how much pressure we can take. What is stimulation for one person produces tension for another. Maryanne felt she had to be occupied all the time. She arrived for appointments puffing and blowing but seemed unconcerned — in fact she appeared to be thriving on multiple arrangements. Pat, on the other hand, felt pressured with too much activity and needed time to prepare herself. In our culture, a great deal of stress results from society imposing unnecessary and unrealistic youth standards on older people. We are led to believe that growing old is something to fight. Hopefully, having read chapter 2 on Myths and Realities, you will be ready to debunk this myth.

ENRICHMENT – TO RESTORE, REFRESH AND MAINTAIN

Like children, grandparents need to explore the things that give pleasure to their bodies, minds and emotions. Being the giver most of the time can be very draining. Steve Biddulph, in his book *The Secret of Happy Children*, talks about an energy tank inside us that has to be filled and maintained. Is your tank running on empty or full? Like a car, if we are not filled we cannot function. Talking to grandparent groups, some ideas developed as to how to live life and to refuel. You probably have many ideas of your own.

How to live life
- One day at a time.
- One task at a time.

- Enjoy leisure and new interests.
- Talk it out. Unburden yourself. Others will welcome your trust.
- Deal with anger by going for a brisk walk or doing something physical. It helps relieve pent-up emotions.
- Say 'no' when you mean it.
- Explore alternative approaches. There may be other ways.
- Be kind to yourself. Reduce self-expectations. Seek out your good points and develop them.
- Take the initiative — make yourself available. Other people may be waiting for you to make the first move.
- Look after your health. Eat nutritious food. Walk three times a week. Get enough sleep.
- Laugh it off — have a sense of humour.
- Exaggerate. What is the most catastrophic thing that can happen to you? This sometimes helps in coping with reality.
- Distance yourself. Will it matter in a few years from now?
- Stay in the present — not in the 'used to be' or 'will be'.
- Don't remind yourself of past mistakes, but forgive yourself again and again.

We often find ourselves spending too many hours in unproductive ways. Then the feeling at the end of the day is one of heaviness and flatness. How often do we let time run away worrying about things that may not happen, looking for lost articles (my car keys were in the washing machine) and getting into situations we would prefer not to be in.

Are you a worrier? If so, try to have a time set aside each day (plus or minus an hour) just to worry as much as you like. This can contain the worry from spilling into the rest of the day. That leaves the rest of your time entirely free for other things. We do not have to be super-grandparents but we can enjoy life and look after ourselves. This means that we will feel more giving to others.

Growth is possible at any age. I learnt to snorkel at 52 and am tackling the computer in my sixties. Peg Phillips started training for an acting career at 65. Now at 75, she is in *Northern Exposure* the television series. Jono, age eight, on being asked what he thought about oldies said, 'The young are famous because they do things, like Michael Jackson who sings. Grandpa should do more carpentry and make more wooden toys then he too could be famous'. Peter, aged six, said that grandparents are lucky. They can do just what they please. Is this a vital message for us?

Pleasure is the key to health. In our society, enjoying oneself is often frowned upon and it is thought that pleasure has to be earned. It also is often thought that pleasure can be enjoyed only if it has a purpose. Bridge is meant to sharpen the mind, dancing to keep us limber, and tennis is meant for social contacts and physical fitness. Does everything that is fun have to serve a useful purpose? Can't activities be enjoyed just for the sheer pleasure?

Jean had many bridge mates. She devised a form for them to fill in as they joined the group. The average age was about 78.

Tick the following:
Single, Married, Widowed, Divorced
Age 70-85
Hearing ....good/fair/poor.
Eyesight ....good/fair/poor.
Memory...good/fair/poor.
Standard...............................excellent/medium/beginner

It didn't really matter what they put — nobody was excluded and they were able to have a good laugh over their infirmities. They were joining together for pure pleasure.

There are two ways we can get enrichment. One is from seeking out pleasurable activities and the other from the joys of grandchildren, families and friends. Joan said that after 60 she discovered talents she never knew she had. She had taken up writing and was publishing a newsletter. At the same time, she joined an art club and was exhibiting her pictures.

Are there people who can enrich your life? Pick up the telephone or write them a letter. Suggest an activity to share or just enjoy the contact.

The following saying is a very wise one: 'To spice our life with pleasure is as important as to season our food.'

SUGGESTIONS FOR ENRICHING ACTIVITIES

- Aerobics, acting, archery, art
- Bridge, boating, bingo, bowls, bushwalking, bicycling, beauty treatments, barber, backgammon, birdwatching
- Cinema, camping, craftwork, concerts, croquet, chess, carpentry, Centre for Continuing Education, collecting—stamps, coins etc
- Dancing, drives, drama
- Exercises, eating, exploring
- Friends, fishing
- Galleries, gardening, games
- Hiking, hairdresser, horseriding, hobbies
- Ice-skating, intellectual stimulation
- Jogging, jacaranda spotting in November
- Kite flying
- Library, lectures, Lion's Club
- Mountaineering, meditating, museums, music, magazines, massage

- Nature, newspapers
- Older Women's Network, oregami
- Picnics, plays, painting, people-watching, politics, photography, pottery, Probus Club
- Questioning, quilting
- Reading, relatives
- Swimming, sailing, strolling, scrabble, snorkelling, socialising, sport, singing
- Television, travelling, tap dancing, theatre, treasures, toy-making
- University of the Third Age
- View Club, visualisation, volunteer work
- Writing, walking, waterskiing, Workers' Educational Association
- Yoga
- Zoo guide

Bill said his most boring time was when he was just sitting doing nothing, or going to his son's and daughter's places when everybody was busy and he was just 'hanging around'. Grandparents need to occupy themselves and realise they have a right to enjoy life. Grandpa John started a course with the University of the Third Age. He said, 'I feel like a six-year-old on the first day of school. I am excited about enrolling and anxious I won't be able to absorb the facts.' He was doing something quite removed from his life of medicine.

Henry Wadsworth Longfellow sums it up in this poem:

> *For age is opportunity no less*
> *Than youth itself, though in another dress.*
> *And as the evening twilight fades away*
> *The sky is filled with stars, invisible by day.*

Love holds the deepest potential for fulfilment and enrichment. Good relationships with family and friends are extremely important.

WHAT MAKES A GOOD RELATIONSHIP?

When several grandparents were asked what makes a good grandparenting relationship, many ideas were suggested. Respect, caring and concern seemed all-important. Involvement without intrusion, and moments to listen and play were objectives. Realising the importance of giving advice only when asked and not making promises if they cannot be fulfilled — and being honest at all times. What about laughter and lots of cuddles? They are important too.

Joys of grandchildren

The great joy from having grandchildren is being able to watch them grow and develop, and to hear their laughter. I vividly remember picking up my grandchildren when they were toddlers so they could reach the garage door handle. Now, they are taller than me and can pick me up. Sharing the big moments of the first smile, first tooth, first word, first step, first day at school, is most exciting. As they grow older, there can be an exchange of stories, interests and jokes. Clare said, 'I have a special joke that only my youngest grandchild and I understand.'

Treats and outings can be very enriching and so can just laughing and talking together. Grandchildren can be very rejuvenating and bring out many talents in their grandparents. Len mentioned how he enjoyed writing poetry for his grandson and he felt inspired just by observing him at play. Marion was encouraged to paint cards for her granddaughter and Cyril entered a photographic exhibition as a result of taking pictures of his family. Being with grandchildren is like going into another world.

F. M. Wightman, a grandmother from *Grandmother's Notebook*, had this to say. 'Speaking as a grandparent, a baby is a prescription to cure depression, a monkey gland for rejuvenation, a substitution for books, television and radio. A baby brings out the love and tolerance which has become rusty with the years.'

This can also apply to older grandchildren who are good company and provide a platform for warm relationships. There is a sense of self-renewal, seeing the world through their eyes. Chris said, 'I enjoy being a grandparent as there is always a future.' Ken found it hard to believe that his granddaughter was working well into the night as a trainee surgeon and could discuss with him all the medical details. It has been noted that grandchildren, through their very existence, can improve the mental health of grandparents. Grandparents, themselves, can grow closer together with their common interest, and can share the caring and love of grandchildren.

Positive memories and treasures

A group of grandparents, when asked to bring their treasures, arrived with armfuls of memories as well. Eena, who had lost all her family because of the war, nominated her 10 grandchildren as her treasures. She had a feeling of fulfilment and warmth in the midst of her large and new family. Many members brought old faded sepia photographs of their parents. It was like a lesson in history, looking at the style of dress and expression and features of the families. Some spoke about old letters and articles — and Joan wore a necklace which was a watch chain handed down from her grandfather to her father, and then to her. The jewellery that quite a few people presented indicated a continuation and regeneration of the family, and a sense of security. It was also something that was easy to carry and use in time of trouble. There were also religous icons, poems and letters, all carrying messages of the past. When Lola's husband died, her 11-year-old grandson wrote a eulogy which she treasured and found most moving. Jean produced a worn-out piece of string which her children used to play cats cradles, and this game is continued today with her grandchildren. Memories and treasures of this kind cannot be taken away, but can live on through the years.

Grandparents can hand down articles with sentimental value to keep alive the memory of a family member who is no longer alive. Kerry, age six, wore a locket. Inside was a photo of her grandmother's parents who she had not known. Granny Meg gave Jason, age 12, his grandfather's coin collection, while Paul, age eight, received his books. I can remember a parcel of scarves arriving for me when my mother died. Her perfume permeated the package.

Memories still linger on when we say, 'She must have got her mathematical ability from Grandpa', or 'he looks just like his grandmother'. The colour of a child's hair, the shape of an ear or foot, a nose, or eyes, can be reminders of ancestors. Those who still live in family homes are constantly living with memories — a chewed-up teddy bear, a well-read school book, or a piece of yellowing lace from great-grandmother's dress, all coming from a bulging attic. I have my father's diary from the Boer War, written when he was 12-years-old. The grandchildren are fascinated by it and when they read it history becomes alive. Also interesting to them is the formal printed card announcing my birth, finished off with a pale pink bow!

In the future, will the family be holding up a well-worn

pair of jeans and a bright-coloured tee shirt, and falling-apart Reebok shoes? What will their memories be of us? Perhaps we need to value any sentimental articles and even label old photographs, so that the next generation can make sense of all those babies and faces of the past. Is this Aunty May or Granny Gerty? We are constantly unravelling dates, people and places on our photographs and slides, not knowing what decade they come from or who they are. What about stamps and coins which need some sorting? Hopefully, apart from sentimental treasures, we will have left behind a legacy of love and trust.

Good relationships with family and friends are all important. There is sometimes a tendency for elders to be inward-looking and to concentrate only on their difficulties and worries. It has been said that 'Life is a banquet and most people starve to death'. We must not let that happen — stretch out to new interests and new lives. We can be a model for our grandchildren to understand what older people are like. When I visited a toyshop with my grandson, there was an animal there called a 'Puggle' which the children adored. He was small and cuddly and his name stood for P-Peace U-Understanding G-Gentleness G-Generosity L-Love and E-Energy. These qualities are often found in grandparents — although the E might be getting a little shaky!

Becoming grandparents may cause an overhaul of relationships between father and son, mother and daughter as you are now on the same level. Adult children become less scornful of the way their parents brought them up and warm feelings can be generated.

Let us hope that Margaret Mead's question and answer concerning some societies isn't altogether true:

Why do grandchildren and grandparents get on so well?
Because they have a common enemy.

Enrichment is all around us just for the taking. We need to stretch out and grasp it. Take time to watch the sunrises and the sunsets, marvel at nature and enjoy relationships with family and other people. At the same time, let us have a healthy regard for ourselves. As Barbra Streisand said, 'No matter what age you are, you have to take the challenge'.

My grandmother is talking on the phone
Ben (8 yrs)

CHAPTER 9

Looking to the Future and Back

We can only guess what will happen in the years to come. As people are living longer, the birth rate is lower and divorce is one in three marriages, the composition of the traditional family unit is changing. In the next 30 years, those over the age of 75 will increase by 120 per cent, and those over 80 by 460 per cent. It has been said that the number of grandparents could exceed the number of grandchildren by the year 2000. Studies predict that, for one reason or another, 20 per cent of women born in the late 1960s will be childless. This could mean that grandparents will have to work harder at their role to protect what they have. Tolerating in-laws and being patient with all the complexities of an extended family might be required of all of us.

GREAT-GRANDPARENTS

When talking to a group of nine-year-olds, I was quite surprised to hear that 5 out of 24 still had great-grandparents. As the children regarded even their grandparents as very old, they were quite amazed if their great-grandparents could walk without sticks! A few of the great-grandparents came from other countries and still only spoke their mother tongue — much to the annoyance of the grandchildren. Tim liked his great-grandmother because she gave him Kit Kats, but, on the whole, there didn't seem to be a great deal of contact between the generations.

In the future, there could be an increase in the number of great-grandparents. This may result in four- to five-generation families. As well as giving continuity to family life it could also create competition between grandparents and great-grandparents. Grandparents may have to give up the grandparenting role to their adult children, in the same way that they had to take a step back when their children became parents.

Zelda, aged 94, said she had two great-grandchildren, but she felt that she had outstayed her welcome and was past her 'use by' date. Her friends were now all in the cemetery. But, she proudly showed me her teeth and said they were natural and told me about all her activities in detail. She certainly still seemed to get a lot out of life and enjoyed her visits to the children, even if sometimes she didn't know if they were great or grand! The Queen Mother is a well known example of a great-grandmother who seems warm, elegant, and a lot of fun. She is often shown with her family and appears to be the consistent thread in a crumbling family.

Maud was the great-grandmother of a very large family. At the age of 90, she gave her twin boys a party for their 70th birthday — there were four generations in attendance. In years to come, it will be possible for great-grandparents to be in their late fifties and sixties, still young and active. Jean, 65, announced that she was to become a great-grandmother. She seemed a little unsure of her role, but felt she had a better relationship with her 21-year-old granddaughter than ever before. Her adult children, however, were quite unready to be grandparents.

Studies have shown that by the year 2000, over 55s could outnumber children under 14. Today, most people would not be able to remember their great-grandparents — nor even their names — and the role of great-grandparent has never really been considered. May be this will be an important generation in the future, and will prove valuable in providing the continuity of life.

BABY-BOOMERS

In the second half of the 1940s, there was a post-war baby boom when men returned from the war and people were full of hope for the future. There was a sense of normality and more certainty about life. The words of a song popular at the time included the line, 'There'll be love and laughter and peace ever after'. People born then would be between 35 and 50 today and will be the grandparents of the future. We need to look at their backgrounds in order to predict what direction grandparenting of the future will take.

The childhood of baby-boomers was very different from a childhood of the Depression, Edwardian or Victorian days. For the baby-boomers there was a sense of security, and children grew up with conservatism. They tended to obey their parents and teachers — who would have been quite authoritarian. As one grandfather said, they were well-mannered and showed respect to their elders. They were another generation of children who should be seen and not heard. Divorce was unusual and children were kept innocent of bad things. It was a softer time than today — safe, drugless and more comfortable. There was little competition, lots of opportunities and less pressure to perform. The pace of life was generally much slower.

Mothers often worked at home providing food, shelter and love, while putting their careers, if they had them, on hold. It was frowned upon if they had any job ideas for themselves and with unpredictable pregnancies common, women were not welcome in the workforce. A great deal was expected of them. As Adrienne Katz says, in her book *The Juggling Act* , "To be a proper wife and mother is to be skilled at cleaning, laundering and baking; sitting quietly, talking problems through, or being understanding, stimulating or fun to be with are activities never to be referred to. At the end of the day, what will a child remember most — a sparkling floor or the good times together?' Homes were to be kept squeaking clean with advertising campaigns promoting health and hygiene. This comes from a fifties' recipe book:

> *A fair start to dinner*
> *Like a fair start to life*
> *Depends very much on the right kind of wife.*

Dad was generally the official breadwinner and didn't necessarily take an active role in the rearing of the children. He usually depended on his wife for the complete running of the home. Boys wore drab clothes and had long hair, while girls were often to be seen in modest, homemade articles. Their hair styles were made up of ringlets, with ribbons or sausage curls. There was no unisex and school children wore hats. Girls were never to be seen without gloves.

There wasn't all the psychology of today and parents struggled through childrearing. I remember carrying Dr Spock (my bible) in one hand, and the baby in the other, trying to figure out how to cope. Truby King had a big influence in enforcing routines, feeding by the clock and being inflexible. Children's needs were considered to be paramount and women were to devote their lives exclusively to the family. Mother love was emphasised by John Bowlby in a popular English paperback *Childcare and the Growth of Love*. This book was helpful in some ways because it focused on the bond between mother and child and emphasised the trauma experienced by sick children going into hospitals, but it led to a belief that it was wrong to leave children and go to work. A feeling of guilt about this is still prevalent today with many women.

Sex was hardly mentioned and there was little information on the subject. In Helen Townsend's book *Baby Boomers*, she says that 'Double beds seemed more like a space-saving device than cradles of passion'. For some, there was still the notion that the stork was responsible for delivering babies. Fathers were chased out of hospitals when their wives were giving birth. This is a far cry from today's attitude when birth is a team effort. It was a time when ecstasy was falling in love and the word gay meant happy and bright. There was a naivete about that era. However, in Australia, there was full employment and an expansion of affluence and economic security.

Perhaps it was all too bland, for in the sixties people started to get bored and restless and thought there must be a lot more to living. With the advent of the pill, there was more freedom, especially for women. Generally, people began to voice their thoughts. Protests over the Vietnam war, nuclear disarmament, the environment and the women's movement accelerated. There was some excitement and stimulation in the air.

Television bridged the distance gap and people became very big consumers as materialism took hold. Travel was within reach of the average person and the world seemed to be getting smaller. In the eighties, a decade known as the 'me' age, computers and technology started to take over. Families began to reduce in size. The new offspring were known as computer babies, who have grown into today's baby busters, knowledgeable in consumerism and business. Once the average family consisted of 3. 2 children — now there is a rate of 2. 1 per family. Parents are very ambitious juggling careers for themselves, as well as caring for families. Job opportunites are fewer, the unemployment rate has hit 11 per cent in Australia, and there is intense competition, even with material things. Who has got the best house, car, sports shoes, computers, and so on? Parents are pressured to educate and care for their children and there are no guarantees or refunds in their upbringing.

YOUNGER GRANDPARENTS

Taking present conditions into consideration, as well as the background of the baby-boomers, let us look to the future. The first of the baby-boomers will be turning 50 in 1995, as the baby-boom time stretched over 25 years starting after the war.

Grandparents of the future could be much younger and play a more parental role than a grandparent one. They will be physically fitter and more active than the previous generation. They will possibly be in the middle of their careers and so will have less time to offer to grandchildren, and less inclination to be babysitters. They will be more self-sufficient and self-reliant with many options. They were a trail-blazing generation, who had very different experiences from their mothers and fathers who often were surrounded by extended family or a network of friends.

Jan was 38 when she became a grandmother. She wasn't at all pleased as she still had a 14-year-old girl at home and was asked to look after the new baby. She felt that neither she, nor her married daughter, were ready for the new role they were to play. On the other hand, Phyllis, 45 and a career person, was delighted. She played the role of granny only when she wanted — and when she was able to offer some time.

It has been said that many women feel fabulous about entering their fifties. They are free of children, feel healthy and are working at their careers. As author Gail Sheehy says, a 'second adulthood' awaits these women. How will grandparenting be for these people who are so enjoying time to themselves? Grandchildren could have very active, energetic and powerful grandparents.

Men often start having new families in their fifties and go through the nappy stage all over again. Sometimes they give more attention to the new family as they realise what they have missed. Jim had remarried and, at 53, had two young daughters as well as a small grandson from his son of a previous marriage. He was pleased, but seemed to put more emphasis on the new parent role. He only saw his grandson occasionally and not on a one-to-one basis. Some young grandparents feel they have been 'pushed' up into another generation before their time and want to retain their youth. They may find it hard to be called grandma or grandpa.

Teenage pregnancies can be catastrophic for parents who are struggling with their ambivalent feelings of anger and joy. They may be faced with rearing their grandchildren and coping with financial burdens, just when they were looking forward to putting their feet up.

BREAKING THE GENDER BARRIER

In the old style of grandparenting, there were set rules as to what part you played. One grandfather, when asked how important this role was for him and how different it was answered, 'only in the sense that I have to sleep with a grandmother'. There were gender differences in that grandfathers were to grandmothers as the breadwinners were to the homemakers at that time. Often the women did the organising and were more verbal, while the men were a bit more reluctant to show their feelings and were often older and less fit. Today, husbands and wives interchange roles and are very versatile in what they do. Men shop, burp babies, and do the washing, while women change the light bulbs, mow the lawn and have demanding careers. Men are free to show emotion and have a domestic commitment while women are not quite as guilty about working outside the home — especially when two pay packets are such a big help, and often essential.

Younger women are forging ahead with their tertiary education. In 1992, there were 69 000 men undergraduates and 87 000 women. In the law and medical faculties, the number of women has gone up to almost 50 per cent. Quite different from the days when education was thought to be a waste of time for women because they would 'just get married and be home makers' In my family, of three boys and a girl, my father was quite shocked when I suggested I go to university. He was even more shocked when I graduated.

Traditionally, women married 'up', to men who were often older and better educated. Will more women remain single and find it difficult to get suitable partners as they ask for equality in careers? Will male partners be younger than before? Who will be the dominant parent in the family? These questions remain unanswered for the moment, but it seems clear that both sexes will be looking for equal partnerships in domestic roles, education, jobs and parenting. This must affect the grandparenting role. Perhaps, as they go into this stage, there will be little difference between grandmothers and grandfathers. They will be more alike and interchangeable. How about Gramps cooking the dinner, making social arrangements, as well as working as a milliner, or infant school teacher. Gran could be laying bricks or continuing her career as an accountant. Anything is possible!

GRANDPARENTING AND PARENTING IN TANDEM

Today there is a high rate of remarriage after divorce. As a result, many grandparents are also the parents of young children. There are twice as many born-again dads as there were 10 years ago. Just as they have got their first children off their hands, they start another family — and possibly do a better job the second time round, having more patience, more time and more appreciation of children.

Paul was divorced and had two adult children, age 20 and 22. He remarried a younger women and had two daughters. While Paul and his wife were having their second baby, his son had a daughter. The three girls enjoy playing together although they do not see each other very frequently. I was in the hospital when my first grandchild was born. Across the passage I saw a man in his seventies, waiting for some good news. I asked confidently, 'Are you waiting for the birth of your grandchild?' 'No' he answered, 'I am expecting a new baby from a second marriage'. The number of adjustments to be made are mindblowing.

This will affect the grandparenting role when two sets of children will be calling you Poppy and Daddy at the same time. Grandchildren and children could also be playing and going to school together. Maybe there will be more of this in the future. Way back in the era of large families, it was not uncommon to be a parent and grandparent simultaneously.

In second marriages, where older men marry much younger women, step-grandparents can be closer in age to their adult step-children. Paul, at 70, married Ann, 28, and they produced two children. Ann is younger than one of Paul's sons from his first marriage. Grandparents, parents and grandchildren can become contemporaries.

There may be serial marriages, with third and fourth marriages not being considered unusual. Already, young people are aghast at anybody who is is married over 20 or 30 years.

OLDER BABY-BOOMER GRANDPARENTS.

Some baby-boomers choose to remain single for longer. They have so many options and can be economically sound and independent. However, at about the age of 30, they may start thinking of their biological clocks. They may consider having their first child in their forties. They have interesting work and now feel more confident of raising happy children without having to be perfect parents. They have decided to work first and do their child-rearing last. This is a reversal from the past.

It appears too that newly-weds are getting older. Here are some figures from the Australian Bureau of Statistics:

Women: In 1972, the average age for marriage is 21
         For 1992, it was 24.7
Men: In 1972, the average for marriage is 23.3
         For 1992, it was 26.9

There is also a decline in the number marrying. This must inevitably delay the onset of grandparenthood.

A heading in a newspaper read 'Boom Baby Boom'. It appears that more than one-third of first births are to women over 30 and that this a very fast-growing group in the community. This might mean that their parents will have to wait longer for their cherished grandchildren to arrive. In these instances, they will be older than other grandparents and their relationships with their grandchildren will be on a different basis and for a shorter duration.

Would there ever be a place for communal living, where grandparents and adult parents have their private living areas but share central services of living? This would compensate for lack of social networks and the end of a large extended family? A yearning for neighbourhood life again — a bit like the 'moshav' in Israel, and the co-housing in Europe and the US which is starting to break the social isolation.

BACK TO THE PRESENT — A NEED FOR GRANDPARENTS

In a world of change, grandchildren need grandparents who can give security, love and continuity. They can gain a lot from the wisdom and knowledge of grandparents, who are also able to give them a great deal of that precious commodity — time. They can absorb values of the past and enjoy the luxury of being heard. One of the most important gifts that grandparents can give to grandchildren is one of unconditional love and an acceptance that is not based on whether they are the fastest runners or top of the class.

Grandparents also help maintain the rituals of birthdays, anniversaries and religious festivities. In this way, they bring the family together. Meg felt she was tired of cooking large meals for celebrations but found that the joy of getting together was greater than her exhaustion. The loner, or the odd one out in the family, is often singled out by grandparents and given the necessary attention and care.

Forming and enriching relationships with the different generations is all important. Respect, love and acceptance mean a lot. Having fun, laughing, and sharing proud moments of small personal triumphs makes the grandparenting role a very special one. As one grandfather said, 'It is a fulfillment in my life. I wish to remain a grandparent for a long time'. Other grandparents have said that it is the best part of their lives.

Grandparenting can bring rich rewards and you experience from the role what you are prepared to contribute. In *The New American Grandparent*, Andrew Cherlin and Frank F. Furstenberg Jr have written, 'Grandparents are not prominent or visible actors in our family system but they are important backstage figures'.

Grandparenthood is also an opportunity to get on an equal footing with adult children, both now being parents in their own ways. Jim said that since he became a grandfather and his daughter a parent, they can talk more openly to each other and have a better relationship — more like colleagues and friends. With the children, there is no relationship of power, but one of affection and warmth. Jess had lots of conflicts with her daughter, particularly when she was going through the teenage stage. When her daughter became a mother, they both seemed to be on the same wavelength and the mother/daughter relationship improved. Grandparenting has a double value. A wonderful opportunity to enjoy the younger generations and, at the same time, a second chance with adult children.

Helpful hints for use with adult children

- Don't treat your adult children as children. They have grown up!
- Give help when possible.
- Go easy on advice. Don't tell them how to parent.
- Listen and talk.
- Don't over-indulge their children. Love is not bought.
- Receive from adult children when they want to give.

TRADITION

The song Tradition from *Fiddler on the Roof* plays on the radio and I am reminded of its importance in family life. The handing down of beliefs, stories, customs and religions can be a very strong force in our lives. For many centuries, older people have been responsible for this. Without it, each generation would have to start all over again. The past can be very powerful in the way it is used — whether it be supportive or destructive.

Religion

Religion can be a huge force in the lives of families. For the Christians, christenings in the traditional lace dress, Holy Communion, Easter and the celebration of Christmas can be enormously important. For the Jewish people, Friday nights, the adherence of the Sabbath and the celebration of Jewish holidays, can bring a sense of belonging.

For other religions throughout the world, traditions have an enormous hold on people.

Food

With food there is a big traditional component. Why is it I continue to make the family recipe for cup cakes? Why am I tentative about watermelon, lest it goes off after one day? (I still hear my mother saying, 'Be careful it can make you sick'. I forget that in her day there was no refrigeration.) Steve Bastoni from the television program *Police Rescue* yearns for gnocchi, just like his grandmother used to make. What about Nanna's apple pie, or the chicken soup which is known to be a cure for all ills. Mary's grandchildren live overseas. She says that every Christmas she makes a Christmas cake and pudding using her grandmother's recipe. She parcels them up and sends them to the other side of the world. Her family expect it every year.

Lena makes a continental vegetable roll every time her family visit. It is filled with all types of vegetables, put in pastry and baked in the oven. They don't want anything else. Ted cooks a lamb leg with onions, carrots, and potatoes. He says that is his complete cooking repertoire and it is a treat for the family.

Songs, stories, customs

Every spring, I fill the house with sweet-smelling freesias. As the perfume wafts through the rooms, my country of origin is brought back to me. One grandmother said she sings songs to her grandchildren which she remembers her mother singing to her grandchildren. The Grand Old Duke of York, and The Red Red Robin Keeps Bob Bob Bobbin' Along are favourites. For some, the songs are in Hebrew, Arabic, Italian, German or French. Sayings like 'She sells seashells on the sea shore', and 'What are the destructions today?' have a special meaning for Joan's family.

Music and fairytales have an important place in many households. *Red Riding Hood, Goldilocks and the Three Bears, Cinderella,* and *The Three Little Pigs* seem to have survived the Jurassic Park era. At bedtime, old lullabies and sayings sometimes do the trick. My mother was a singer. She made one record before marrying and giving up her career to raise her family. I found myself humming the Brahms *Lullaby* when my children were babies. 'Early to bed, early to rise, makes a man healthy, wealthy and wise' is another old saying to encourage children to bed. I have to admit, it doesn't have a great chance of working in today's world.

One grandfather said he and his grandson have a secret password, originating from his paternal grandfather, that only the two of them know. This has created a very deep feeling between them. Lots of games have been handed down. I Spy can be just as effective on a long journey as a Gameboy. What about Simon Says, Happy Families, Old Maid, Cats Cradles, Battleships, Dot-to-Dot, Hangman, and the like? Beth, 4, and Amy, 12, played with the basket of scarves which had been in the family for years. They named it Scarfomania and set up a shop which occupied them for many hours. Dress-up boxes, with clothes of the past, conjure up old traditions and stories.

Tradition in parenting

It is interesting to see how a great deal is learnt about parenting from one generation to another. I often notice some of my adult children's responses to their children being similiar to mine. Sometimes this is rather unnerving when I have made a hash of things. On the other hand, I am thrilled when it works well. Dorothy says she hears her daughter using the same expression, 'I've had enough, stop it'. Anna, who is of Italian origin, baths her baby in the kitchen. For her, that was where the life of the house took place and she saw all the family action. The memories from adult children's own nurseries are often carried along. Some say, 'I don't want to be like my parents'. Others say, 'I want to do something different'.

Even in dressing, grandmother Meg said she never wears red because her mother said it was vulgar. On the other hand, Libby is constantly regailed in purple, rebelling against the negative messages of the old days. Little did she realise that it was the popular colour of the suffragettes.

Tradition can also be very frightening. In the book *Like Water for Chocolate* by Laura Esquivel, we meet a Mexican family from the beginning of the century, whose youngest daughter traditionally must not get married, but stay at home and look after mother. Great anguish and tragedy ensures. In some societies it is traditional for women to be chaperoned and have their husbands selected for them. In some families, the eldest son must stay behind or follow in the business and academic footsteps of the father – the women do not warrant educating. This can also cause conflict in the modern world.

The past has an enormous power so we have to find a way to be loving and caring models. In the book *Touchpoints* Dr T. Berry Brazelton, an American paediatrician, says, 'Family and cultural traditions can be an important base for a child's self-image. I would urge new parents to treasure traditional ways'. Tradition can be of great significance as long as it is not enforced on anybody. It adds to the continuity of the different generations and seems to strengthen the link in the chain of life.

HOPE FOR CHANGE

Society will change. In the end, hopefully, there will be no age discrimination and a higher regard for grandparents and older people, especially as the baby-boomers go into this generation. In the childrens' book *Our Granny*, Margaret Wild has depicted grandmothers in a most positive and active way. She not only mentions the conventional activities grannies would be doing, like babysitting, but also the more unconventional, like truck driving, plumbing, university study, writing books, playing in a band or working in an office. This can equally apply to grandfathers and is a far cry from rocking chairs and walking sticks. Perhaps grandchildren in the 21st century will say, 'my grandmother is an oil-tanker engineer and my grandfather is a family planning nurse'! Maybe the next generation will prepare themselves ahead of time for entering the later years and taking on the role of grandparenting. This role may be more clearly defined by the grandparents themselves, who will decide what they wish to give and what they do not want to be in on. As one grandparent says, 'I get exasperated when I have too much grandparenting and annoyed when I don't have enough'. She may be able to clarify this for herself in the future. It appears that already grandparents are making unwritten contracts with their grandchildren and choosing what jobs they will do and what role they will play.

And could it be that our society will value the role of both parenting and grandparenting much more? Society may be more child-centred, where everybody takes responsibility for the children in our world, not just the parents. In this way, they may be free to walk the path of life in safety, and feel valued and loved — rather different from our somewhat disposable and soulless society. There will be intergenerational programs and families will be of national concern. Relationships will be enriched and there will be no need to call the young ankle-biters or kids (they are not goats), or older people, oldies and wrinklies.

Hopefully, the media will depict grandparents in a truer way. They are human beings who are simply further on in the life continuum and have lots of love and caring to offer to others, as well as to themselves. At the same time, we have to stop seeing ageing as an enemy and enjoy grandparenthood. Growing old is really an ongoing project of self-actualisation. Penelope Leach in *Children First* says, 'Children are the responsibility of us all. They are a large part of our present and certainly of everybody's future.'

Mary, 100, a great-great-grandmother who is creating quite a few firsts, swam 50 metres in four minutes. She said her secret was, 'that she didn't smoke, drink, swear or go out with bad men', and didn't know what all the media fuss was all about. It seems there was more to it than that. Perhaps she had drunk from Betty Freidan's 'Fountain of Age', which is becoming a catchcry for the older generation.

EXTENDED FAMILY

It seems that the extended family is coming back into fashion again. Young people are staying at home longer because of high unemployment and because the expense of living away is very great. Betty mentioned she had to cook a nourishing meal for her 23-year-old son who had exams, while at the same time, looking after her grandson of 2 when the parents were at work. She also provided free accomodation and financial support for her son and gave many hours of her time in grandchild care. Quite a formidable task! A survey done by the Australian Bureau of Statistics, in 1992, showed that women do most of the caring in families. In fact, they are known as the women in the middle. They may have an elderly parent to look after, a retiring husband, adult children and grandchildren. With the latter, there can be three sets of obligations — step-grandchildren, own grandchildren and new sets. The mind boggles again, for on top of all this they have themselves to look after. Relatives generally are responsible for a great deal of childcare and, in 43 per cent of cases, grandma is the one who comes to the rescue. How many millions of dollars are saved by all this unpaid work?

In California, programs are starting to aquaint grandparents with bringing up babies nineties' style. So much has changed in parenting methods. In Australia, Tresillian are also offering courses for grandparents.

The demand to look after families has become greater as older people live longer and sometimes need both practical and emotional help, particularly in times of sickness. Households can be made up of three and sometimes four generations. Eighty eight per cent of Australians share a home with at least one other family member who is related by blood, an in-law or fostered. So it seems that the extended family is extremely active again, providing not only affection and support, but also practical and financial help.

Perhaps by starting with the family and relationships, we can move towards trust and affection rather than force and obedience. Dictatorship and stereotypes often lead to wars. We cannot afford to put grandparents on the scrapheap but need to draw upon the resources of each generation. We can learn from others' experiences and assist each other. Timothy Leary, a radical in the sixties, was telling people to go and help someone from a previous generation to 'turn on', to wake up to the beauty of life and of themselves. Family ties are strong and mostly binding.

Grandparents, adult children and grandchildren can lead us to a better world by enriching their relationships. It takes a lot of thought, time and energy but adds another dimension to our lives.

As there are more grandparents alive today than at any time in history, we can have a big impact. Being honest, showing love and care, can help grandchildren as they climb the tree of life. At the same time we can enrich our own lives and continue to take up a 'new challenge'.

> *There are two lasting bequests*
> *we can give our children.*
> *One of these is roots;*
> *the other wings.*
> **Hodding Carter**

A trendy grandma with high hair and earrings
Josh (6 yrs)

Sayings of Grandchildren

1. A good thing about not having grandparents is you don't have to be sad and go to their funeral. (10 yrs)
2. I feel sad not having them in the holidays to go to the park. (10 yrs)
3. They give me money, books, icecream, lollies and love. (9 yrs)
4. My grandparents are so shy. They never question anything I want. (12 yrs)
5. My Nanna is so strict at times and that's what I don't like about her. Sometimes I get mad and feel I could cut her in half like a piece of toast. (8 yrs)
6. My Nanna gives me lots of presents which are really so nice. She helps me clean my room and sometimes helps me garden. (10 yrs)
7. My Gran is game to do everything. She even goes boogie boarding and then her costume balloons up and we have to rescue her. (13 yrs)
8. Gran, you look the same in old photos except now you have wrinkles. (7 yrs)
9. I don't want to be older than 40. You'd get exhausted just standing up. (10 yrs) (From Christine Harris *Trees in my Ears*)
10. I like it when Nana tells me what my mother did when she was little. I always remember her stories because she tells them over and over again. (10 yrs) (From *Trees in my Ears*)
11. A grandfather told his grandson that when he was older

he would move into the granny flat under the house. The grandson replied 'Gramps, you are old already.' (8 yrs)

12. Gran blows the biggest soap bubbles, bakes the yummiest cakes and talks for hours on the phone. (11 yrs)
13. My grandfather always has a joke. He has a great ability in Scrabble and a second-to-none ability of the English language. He knows so many words that they haven't quite made it to the dictionary. (11 yrs)
14. Have you any Beatrix Potter books Gran? She would have been 100-years-old — not much older than you. (6 yrs)
15. One bad thing with Gran and Gramps, you have to walk slowly and behave when you go out. (9 yrs)
16. Gran, when you go skiing, you have to wear a neck-warmer, ear-warmer and a mouth-warmer. Your face may freeze. (12 yrs)
17. My Gran did a lot for me and then last year she died. I went to her funeral. I really miss her, so does Grandpa I think. (10 yrs)
18. My Grandpa can sleep and watch television at the same time. (9 yrs)
19. My Nan is 70. She doesn't get angry or selfish and she has a good sense of humour. She plays tennis, croquet and bridge. (11 yrs)
20. My Nana worries all the time. She worries about the dog and the flowers. She gives me lots of presents which are so nice. (9 yrs)
21. My grandparents live far away. They send me letters with pretty paper. On my birthday, they send me a card with 30 dollars. On their birthdays, I send some yummy chocolates tied with a red and green bow. (8 yrs)

22. It must be wonderful being grandparents. You can get up late in the morning, eat whatever you like and nobody tells you what to do. (13 yrs)
23. My Nana has freckles on her hands and face. She knits and sews for me. (7 yrs)
24. My Gramps is a good driver and he makes things in his carpentry room. (6 yrs)
25. It is good fun with Gran and Gramps. They take us to dinner and laugh with us. (5 yrs)
26. My grandparents are my biggest fans. They encourage me and seem to understand me very well, even when I have my bad days. (10 yrs)
27. My Nana is blonde, blue-eyed and she wears glasses. She is very quiet and doesn't scream at me when I do something wrong. (9 yrs)
28. I like my Gramp because he was the first relative to hold me when I was born. He is strong and brave. (9 yrs)
29. I wish my Gran wouldn't answer her own questions. What is 48+93? She answers 141. (8 yrs)
30. My Gramps is a good sailor and on the boat I had the best soup I have ever had in my life. (9 yrs)
31. Grandparents get very tired very quickly. They go to bed very early. (8 yrs)
32. My grandfather is very cranky. When we go in the car he says 'Keep quiet'. (8 yrs)
33. My Nana has hair that sticks up. She has gold in her teeth. (5 yrs)
34. My Nana brings afternoon tea to school everyday. I wish she would ask me what I want, like tarts and cakes. (8 yrs)
35. Grandpa has no hair. The wind blew it away. (5 yrs)
36. I like to go to Gramps and Gran to study before exams.

It is quiet and my brothers can't annoy me. I also have my favourite foods. (13 yrs)

37. When I go to Nana's she says, 'Just remember when you're here and your mum is away, I'm the boss. You can do anything you want because I'm in charge'. (9 yrs)
38. Sometimes I pretend to murder my grandfather, especially when he shouts at me. (11 yrs)
39. My grandmother does not know how to turn the television button. She ends up watching cartoons. (10 yrs)
40. My grandfather is so frustrated that his head has blown off. He is fighting with Granny. (10 yrs)
41. It is so nice to have a grandmother to grumble to. (7 yrs)
42. A grandmother corrects your grammar and wipes imaginary dirt from your cheeks. (12 yrs)
43. A grandfather asked to speak to Jess' father. She shouted, 'Your dad and my Papa is on the phone'. (4 yrs)

Jokes and Riddles from the Grandchildren

Q: What do you get when you cross an owl and a skunk?
    A: *A smelly animal that doesn't give a hoot.*

Q: What lives in Jurassic Park and has a fantastic vocabulary?
    A: *A Rogerthesaurus.*

Q: Why is a snail so smart?
    A: *Because you can't pull its leg.*

Q: What was wrong with the cross-eyed teacher?
    A: *He had trouble with his pupils.*

Q: What is white when dirty?
    A: *A blackboard.*

Q: What kind of cat is found in a library?
    A: *A catalogue.*

Q: Why did the chicken cross the playground?
    A: *To get to the other slide.*

Q: Why couldn't Cinderella play in the football team?
    A: *Because she had to run away from the ball.*

Q: What is the difference between a fish and a piano?
    A: *You can't tuna a fish.*

Q: What do people do in clock factories ?
    A: *They make faces all day.*

Q: Who took Bo Peep's sheep?
    A: *The crook she had.*

Q: Knock, knock. who's there?
    A: *Booo*
    Boo who?

Q: Knock, knock, who's there?
    A: *Cook*
    Cook who?

Q: When is the vet busiest?
    A: *When it rains cats and dogs.*

Q: Why is a dentist moody?
    A: *Because he always looks down in the mouth.*

Q: What happened when the dog swallowed the watch?
    A: *He got a lot of ticks.*

Q: What did the snails do when they got together?
    A: *They slugged each other.*

Q: What kind of instrument does a skeleton play?
    A: *A trombone.*

Q: Why did the kid put his head on the piano?
    A: *Because he wanted to play by ear.*

Q: What fish is famous?
    A: *A starfish.*

Q: Where do animals go when they lose their tails?
    A: *To a retail store.*

Q: Why is the sand wet?
    A: *Because the sea weed.*

Q: Why are spiders like tops?
   A: Because they are always spinning.

Q: When do mathematicians die?
   A: When their numbers are up.

Q: What has a big mouth but doesn't say a word?
   A: A river.

Q: What remains stationary no matter how much you move it?

   A: Writing paper.

Q: What stays hot in the fridge?
   A: Mustard.

My Nan answering her own questions
Oliver (9 yrs)

Questionnaire on Grandparenting

Please fill in the form in any way you choose. There is no right or wrong.

1. What are you thoughts and feelings about being a grandparent?

   ....

2. What do you think makes a good grandparent?

   ....

3. Do you get too little or too much time — or just the right time with your grandchildren?

   ....

4. How often have you wanted to express a difference of opinion on parenting with your adult children? Have you done so, or not?

   ....

5. What do you like to do with your grandchildren?

   ....

6. Are there special family recipes, jokes, common expressions or songs handed down through the family? Can you describe one?

   ....

7. Are there mutual or special events that bring the family together, e.g. birthdays, anniversaries? What are they like?

   ....

8. How different are things today from when you had grandparents?

   ....

9. Do you get on with your in-laws or not? What do you think makes a good relationship with them?

   ....

10. Any other comments regarding the role of grandparents?

    ....

Questionnaire for Grandchildren

1. What is it like to have grandparents, or someone you are especially close to?

   ....

2. What do you call your grandmother and grandfather?

   ....

3. What do you like to do with your grandparents?

   ....

4. What kind of places do you like to go to with them?

   ....

5. What do you think grandparents' lives are like?

   ....

6. Do grandparents teach you anything? What do you teach them?

   ....

7. What is the funniest thing that has ever happened to your grandpa or grandma?

   ....

8. What memories do grandparents share with you?

   ....

9. Do your grandparents ever get sad or angry? How do you feel about that?

....

10. Do you want to say anything else about them? How they look? How they laugh? What they do?

....

Useful Organisations

For contact telephone numbers and addresses of the following organisations, please check your local telephone directory.

Alzheimers Associations (Australia)

Art Gallery of NSW

Australian College for Seniors, University of Wollongong

Bereavement Care Centre

Carers' Association of NSW

Combined Pensioners Association of NSW

Council on the Ageing (Cota)

Continuing Education (at your local university)

Family Court

Law Society

Lions Club

National Retirement Association

National Heart Foundation

National Trust

Older Women's Network

Probus Centre

Retirement Advisory Service

Retirement Village Association

Rotary

R.S.V.P. Volunteer Centre

University of the Third Age

View Clubs of Australia

Voluntary Euthanasia Society

WEA Adult Education

Suggested Reading

Dr Alex Comfort *A Good Age* Pan Books

Steve Biddulph *Secret of Happy Children* Bay Books

Robert Aldrich & Glenn Austin *Grandparenting for the 90s* Robert Erdmann Publishing

Christine Harris *Trees in my Ears* Wakefield Press

Dr T. Berry Brazelton *Touchpoints* Doubleday

Leila Friedman *Why Can't I Sleep at Nana's Anymore?* Match Books

Betty Freidan *The Fountain of Age* Jonathan Cape

Thomas Gordon *Parent Effectiveness Training in Action* Bantam Books

Elizabeth Kubler-Ross *On Death & Dying* Tavistock Publications

Mal McKissock *Coping with Grief* ABC Enterprises

Andrew Cherlin & Frank Furstenberg *The New American Grandparent* Harvard Press

Dorothy Corkille Briggs *Your Child's Self-Esteem* Doubleday Dolphin

Rosemary Wells *Your Grandchild & You* Sheldon Press

Nell Dunn *Grandmothers* Chatto & Windus

Eena Job *Fending Off Forgetfulness* University of Queensland Press

Manuel Smith *When I Say No I Feel Guilty* Bantam

Virginia Satir *Peoplemaking* Palo Alto California

Herbert Benson *Relaxation Response* Fountain

In Praise of Grandmothers Running Press Miniature Edition

Felstin *Sex in Later Life* Pelican

Dargott/Kalish *A Time to Enjoy the Pleasures of Aging* Prentice Hall

Louise Hay *You can Heal Yourself* Specialist Publications

Ainslie Meares *The Silver Years* Greenhouse Publications

Jorge Ward and Muriel James *Born to Win* Signet New American Library

Eda Le Shan *Grandparents – A Special Kind of Love* Macmillan (13+Adult)

Penelope Leach *Baby & Child* Penguin

Penelope Leach *Children First* Michael Joseph

Jane Adams *I'm Still Your Mother* Delacorte

books on grandparents for children

The most appropriate age group is given in parentheses

Paul Jennings Peter Gouldthorpe *Granddad's Gifts* Penguin (8+)

Phoebe Gilman *Something from Nothing* (Jewish Folk Tale) Ashton (5+)

Nate Hilton *The Web* Young Blue Gum (8-12)

John Burningham *Grandpa* Picture Puffin (3-5)

Barry Dickins *My Grandfather* Penguin (9+)

Barry Dickins *My Grandmother* Penguin (9+)

Ann Scott & M. Kelleher Aubrey *Grandmother's Chair* (5+)

Penny Robenstone *Grandma's Knee* Heinemann (4+) (About death)

Bryan Mellanie & Robert Ingpen *Lifetimes* Puffin (4+) (About death)

Margaret Wild Julie Vivas *Our Granny* Omnibus (5+)

Barbara Pollard *Grandma and Grandpa are Special People* Celestial Arts (5+)

Diana Kidd *The Day my Grandma Came to Stay* Angus & Robertson (8+)

Bob Graham *Granddad's Magic* Puffin (4+)

Valerie Flournay *Patchwork Quilt* Puffin/Penguin (5+)

Margaret Gordon *Grandpa's Slide Show* Puffin/Penguin (5-8)

Donna Guthrie *Grandpa Doesn't Know It's Me* Human Sciences Press Inc New York. (In co-operation with Alzheimers Disease and Related Disorders Association) (6+)

Dianne Bates *Grandma Cadbury's Trucking Tales* Bluegum (9+)

Dianne Bates *Grandma Cadbury's Safari Tours* Bluegum (9+)

Babette Cole *The Trouble with Grandad* Little Mammoth (3+)

BIBLIOGRAPHY

Aldrich & Glenn Austin *Grandparenting in the 90s* (1991) Robert Erdmann Pub

Biddulph Steve *The Secret of Happy Children* (1984-1993) Bay Books

Bowlby John *Childcare & the Growth of Love* World Health Organisation report (1952/3)

Brazelton T. Berry *Touchpoints* (1992) Doubleday

Briggs Dorothy Corkille *Your Child's Self-esteem* (1970-1975) Doubleday-Dolphin

Cherlin Andrew & Furstenberg Frank Jnr *The New American Grandparent* (1986) Harvard Press

Conolly Joy *Step families* (1983) Corgi

Dahl Roald *George's Marvellous Medicine* (1986) Puffin

Esquivel Laura *Like Water for Chocolate* (1993) Doubleday

Edgar Don No.25 Dec. '89 *Family Matters* Children, Youth, Elders, Rethinking the generations

Friedman Leila *Why can't I sleep at Nana's anymore?* (1990) Matchbooks

Friedan Betty *Fountain of Age* (1993) Jonathan Cape

Gordon Thomas *Parent Effectiveness Training* (1970-1979)

Horin Adele 'Granny to the Rescue When Crisis Hits' *Sydney Morning Herald* Dec.15th 1992

Harris Christine *Trees in my Ears* (1992) Wakefield

Job Eena *Fending off Forgetfulness* (1985) University of Queensland Press

Kahlil Gibran *The Prophet* (1923-62) Borzoi Books

Katz Adrienne *The Juggling Act* (1992) Bloomsbury

Kidd Diana *The Day Grandma Came to Stay* (and spoilt my life) (1988-1992) Angus & Robertson

Kubler Ross Elizabeth *On Death & Dying* (1969) Collier

Laslett Peter *A Fresh Map of Life: The Emergence of the Third Age* Harvard University Press (Reference to four stages of life in Chapter 2)

Mellanie Bryan Ingpen Robert *Beginnings & Endings with Lifetimes in Between* (1983) Hill of Content, (1986) Puffin

McKissock Mal *Coping with Grief* (1985) ABC Enterprises

Park Ruth *Fishing in the Styx* (1993) Viking

Scott Herbert Ann, Kelleher Meg *Grandmother's Chair* (1990) Clarion Books

Townsend Helen *Baby Boomers* (1988) Simon & Schuster

Wild Margaret, Vivas Julie *Our Granny* (1993) Omnibus

Wells Rosemary *Your Grandchild and You* (1991) Sheldon Press

Wightman F.M. *Grandmother's Notebook* Journal by Juliette Clarke (1992) Exley Publications